A CENTURY OF WAR

A CENTURY OF WAR

LINCOLN, WILSON, AND ROOSEVELT

JOHN V. DENSON

Ludwig
von Mises
Institute
AUBURN, ALABAMA

JOHN V. DENSON practiced law as a defense trial attorney for many years and in 1988 was inducted into the American College of Trial Lawyers. In 2005, he was elected Circuit Judge. He is the editor of and a contributor to two prior books, *The Costs of War: America's Pyrrhic Victories* and *Reassessing the Presidency: The Rise of the Executive State and the Decline of Freedom*. All proceeds from the sale of this book go to the Ludwig von Mises Institute in Auburn, Alabama.

"A Century of War" was delivered as a lecture in 1997 at the fifteenth anniversary of the Ludwig von Mises Institute. "Abraham Lincoln and the First Shot" and "Franklin D. Roosevelt and the First Shot" are from *Reassessing the Presidency: The Rise of the Executive State and the Decline of Freedom* (Auburn, Ala.: Mises Institute, 2001). "The Calamity of World War I," and "Another Century of War?" first appeared in the *Freeman*, and "The Will to Peace" was originally published on LewRockwell.com and Mises.org.

Front cover: Photo by Frank Hurley. Permission granted by the Australian War Memorial, negative number E01220.

ISBN: 10 digit: 1-933550-06-6
ISBN: 13 digit: 978-1-933550-06-0

THIS BOOK IS DEDICATED TO the courageous individuals who will struggle against the odds, certain vested interests, and the power of the State to create a will to peace in the twenty-first century.

ACKNOWLEDGMENT

I would like to thank, Donna Moreman, for all the extra hours she has worked, in addition to her regular duties as my legal secretary, in order to type speeches, books, and lectures. I also want to thank Judy Thommesen, with the Ludwig von Mises Institute, who served as editor for this book and for her wise counsel and helpful suggestions. Thanks also to Chad Parish, with the Mises Institute, for the cover design that so vividly shows the horrors of war. Finally, I want to thank Lew Rockwell, not only for his friendship since we met in 1982, but for his commitment to Mrs. Ludwig von Mises to create the Mises Institute and to devote his life to promoting the ideas of her brilliant husband. The Mises Institute has been a fantastic success and I am very proud to have been associated with it since the beginning.

Contents

PREFACE

THE TWENTY-FIRST CENTURY MUST take the path less traveled and reverse the direction taken in the war-torn twentieth century, the bloodiest in history. When the First World War, where ten million soldiers were killed, evolved into the Second World War, where fifty million people were killed, we experienced the concept of total war. A large percentage of the fifty million were civilians (women and children) killed by British and American aircraft which dropped bombs on nonmilitary targets in order to demoralize the enemy. In other words, the end justified the means.

The Second World War ended with the first atomic bombs being dropped on Japan, despite the fact that for months Japan had been offering to surrender if they could keep their Emperor. This offer was refused because of Roosevelt's unconditional surrender policy which Truman also adopted. After America dropped the bombs, and after Russia had been in the war for six days, we accepted their surrender and let the Japanese keep their Emperor.

The war was followed by the Nuremberg and Tokyo trials which established, for the future, that the political and military leaders who lose a war will be tried by the victors and then executed. This established the pattern that no military or political leader will be *willing* to lose a war, therefore ensuring it will escalate into a total war to avoid losing and being executed.

The twenty-first century, I believe, will be the nuclear century since this amazing source of energy, i.e., uranium, holds the promise of future prosperity for the rapidly growing industrialized world. However, if nuclear power is used in a total war, we literally face the possible extinction of the human race, or at least the destruction of Western Civilization.

We must learn to avoid war and develop a general will to peace. I believe the key to this development is to learn the truth about the real causes and effects of wars so that we can see through the false propaganda which is used by political leaders to convince us to go to war.

I am advocating the careful study of history for the purpose of developing this will to peace. One of my favorite history professors is Ralph Raico who tells the story of asking his college students, "What is history?" and one of the students replied, "It's just one damn thing after another." Henry Ford said, "History is bunk," meaning that it is usually false and misleading rather than unimportant when correctly written. In Ambrose Bierce's *Devil's Dictionary*, he defined history as "an account, mostly false of events mostly unimportant, which are brought about by rulers, mostly knaves, and soldiers, mostly fools." However, when history is written truthfully I believe that Bolingbroke gave the best definition, "History is philosophy teaching by example." If we can read history by looking at past events to determine what ideas were being followed, we can see how those ideas worked out in practice and learn lessons from the experience of others and avoid the same mistakes. The extreme importance of history and its study was cogently stated by Patrick Henry, "I have but one lamp by which my feet are guided, and that is the lamp of experience. I know of no other way of judging the future but by the past."

The big question about history is usually "What are the true facts?" You cannot always rely on eyewitnesses since they may have a bias. Sometimes diaries and writings made contemporaneously are true but are not found for many years, decades, or centuries. It is almost impossible for history to be written without the writer's judgment or bias being expressed in the form of an interpretation. Therefore, history is always evolving and it is always subject to revision by better and more reliable evidence.

This brings us to the controversial question of "What is revisionism?" Usually when some establishment position is questioned as to its authenticity and a new version is proposed, it is condemned as "revisionism" or an effort to distort the truth, when in fact, the revisionism may state the correct facts. The best definition of revisionism was stated by one of America's foremost revisionist historians, Harry Elmer Barnes, "Revisionism is bringing history into accord with the facts." In George Orwell's famous novel *Nineteen Eighty-Four* he depicts "revisionism" as a word of opprobrium and demonstrates it with the governmental department entitled "The Ministry of Truth" where history is intentionally falsified to obscure the past because people who do not know the truth about the past, and cannot learn lessons from history, are more easily controlled by the government, not only in the present, but for the future. Therefore, when the word revisionism is used, it must be determined in what context it is being used, i.e., whether the definition stated by Barnes, or in the sense of George Orwell's novel.

One of the most dramatic examples of true revisionism concerns the "Donation of Constantine." This was a document widely circulated for centuries throughout Western Civilization which was alleged to be a document composed by the Emperor Constantine (272–337) which made a gift of Rome and the western part of the Roman Empire to Pope Sylvester while the eastern part of the empire was established at the capital of Constantinople. This alleged donation constituted the cornerstone of the papal claim for both religious and secular power in Rome, which is one of the reasons, for instance, that Charlemagne traveled to Rome to be crowned as emperor by the Pope on Christmas day in 800. It was not until the fifteenth century that Lorenzo Valla (1407–57) exposed this document as a complete forgery, thereby causing tremendous repercussions in Western Civilization from that time forward relating to both the secular and papal sovereignty and power of Rome.

It is in regard to war, however, that most revisionism becomes necessary because truth is almost always the first casualty of war. In most wars throughout history, the political leaders first need to gain the support of the citizens who must fight, pay taxes, and sacrifice their lives. To obtain popular approval leaders have often used false propaganda to state the reasons for the war. False propaganda often continues throughout the war to instill hatred of the enemy and finally, it is used at the end to prove that it was a just war, thereby justifying the sacrifices made by the citizens. Since winners write the history, the false propaganda used from the beginning to the end is often accepted as the true history of the war.

One clear and dramatic incident relating to war and "good revisionism" was an incident known as the Katyn Forest massacre which was used during World War II, and in many history books since that date, to show the Germans' atrocities. The Katyn Forest is located in modern-day Belarus. In September of 1939 both Germany and the Soviet Union invaded Poland and occupied it jointly. It was reported later that thousands of Polish army officers, political leaders, intellectuals, and teachers had been rounded up, massacred, and buried in mass graves. In 1943 a grave was discovered which contained over 15,000 of these missing persons, piled on top of each other and each had a single bullet hole in the back of the head. The wartime propaganda of America, the British, and the Soviets was that the Germans were guilty of this atrocity. The graves of the remaining persons have never been disclosed or discovered.

This allegation of mass murder helped to fuel hatred toward the Germans, as did other false allegations, all clearly revealed in *The Propaganda Warriors: America's Crusade Against Nazi Germany* by Clayton D. Lauria and *'Twas a Famous Victory: Deception and Propaganda in the War Against Germany*, by Benjamin Colby. During the 1970s and 80s I read various accounts that cast doubt about the truth of the wartime propaganda relating to the Katyn Forest massacre. But it was not until 1989 that Soviet leader Mikhail Gorbachev produced the actual documents which revealed conclusively that the Soviet secret police, under the specific orders of Joseph Stalin in 1940, murdered 21,587 Polish enemies of the Soviet state and buried most of them in this particular grave. Gorbachev did not reveal any documents showing the location of the remaining graves.[1]

---

[1]The plaque at this grave site blaming the Germans for the Katyn Forest atrocity was removed once this information was made known.

The false propaganda against the Germans in World War I is shown in detail by an excellent book entitled *Falsehood in Wartime: Propaganda Lies of the First World War* by Arthur Ponsonby, a member of the British Parliament. False propaganda was also employed by government officials leading up to and during World War II. A study of the false propaganda in World War II shows that no lie was too large to prevent its use against Hitler and no crime of Stalin was too large to prevent its being hidden from the American public.

We now know since new documents have been discovered by the research of R.J. Rummel and revealed in his books *Death by Government* and *Power Kills* that Stalin was the world's foremost murderer and that Mao of China was number two, making communism the deadliest political philosophy in all history. At the end of World War II far more people were living under tyranny than before the war. This tyranny was communism. However, the war was labeled as a great victory over tyranny because of the defeat of Hitler.

One of the purposes of this book is to show the importance of revisionism because I believe it is one of the main keys to developing a general will to peace for the future. The following essays were written at various times and for different purposes, i.e., book reviews, a speech, and then articles for books. They all relate to history primarily involving the real causes of war as well as the actual results. A study of history like this, I believe, will help make people more aware of the fabricated propaganda that appears as history today, not only in the history books, but often in the news media about the causes and the effects of war. Americans, in particular, seem to be very naïve about the real causes and effects of wars and tend to accept at face value the reasons given by politicians. If Americans would be more skeptical and question the reasons given by politicians to enter into war, and further insist that only Congress can declare war (which the Constitution specifically requires), rather than letting presidents get us into wars, we will see fewer wars. Also, if history is studied to understand the *real* causes and effects of war and the loss of freedom that results even in winning a war, this would increase that skepticism.

An excellent introduction to revisionism can be obtained by reading a book by Harry Elmer Barnes entitled *Revisionism: A Key to Peace and Other Essays*, which was published by the Cato Institute in 1980. Another good introduction to the subject is James J. Martin's *Revisionist Viewpoints: Essays in a Dissident Historical Tradition*. These books will introduce the reader to many other detailed histories which delve into the real background of American wars. Much excellent research has been done and published, but the public-at-large is not aware of these books because there are certain gatekeepers such as the Council on Foreign Relations, who have reasons to prevent this knowledge from reaching the general public.

After World War I there was a tremendous amount of revisionism showing the false propaganda used by President Wilson and others to get America into that war. After the war a thorough investigation also showed there were certain economic interests of bankers and munition makers who encouraged the war for their own financial profit, which was the first real indication of the industrial-military-banking complex. Congressional investigations that followed exposed the abuse of power that took America into World War I and resulted in the Neutrality Acts being passed to try to prevent future unnecessary or unjust American wars.

By the time of the attack on Pearl Harbor on December 7, 1941, public opinion polls showed that over 80 percent of the American public was opposed to entering another European war. It took the dramatic event of the attack on Pearl Harbor to shift public opinion overwhelmingly to support our entry into the war. The public was unaware of the evidence that we now have that Roosevelt had provoked the attack on Pearl Harbor and actually withheld information from the military commanders stationed there, which, if furnished to them, would have probably prevented the attack. There is also much excellent revisionist history that President Lincoln provoked the firing on Fort Sumter for economic reasons having nothing to do with the abolition of slavery. Two essays in this book address these subjects of provoking the first shot in some detail.

As Americans become aware of this revisionist history, it could very well create a general will to peace. There are some hopeful signs that the gatekeepers will not be able to prevent revisionist history from reaching the general public because of the internet. Of course, the internet can contain false as well as truthful information, so much discretion will be required. Another hopeful sign is the use of the Freedom of Information Act. One of the best and most recent disclosures of Roosevelt's acts provoking the attack at Pearl Harbor is contained in a book published in the year 2000 entitled *Day of Deceit: The Truth about FDR and Pearl Harbor* by Robert D. Stinnett which is discussed fully in the essay on Roosevelt which follows herein. Stinnett's book is dedicated to the late Congressman, John Moss (D., CA) who was the author of the Freedom of Information Act and Stinnett states that without this Act, "the information revealed in this book would never have surfaced."

Finally, the last essay in this book is about the Christmas Truce in which the German and British soldiers realized that by the first Christmas of World War I, they could not figure out why they were fighting each other. The soldiers, on both sides of the trenches, in direct disregard of orders not to fraternize with the enemy, and probably facing certain court-martial for their actions, put down their arms and celebrated Christmas together in 1914. When the officers saw that they could not prevent the Christmas celebration they joined with the soldiers. The entire twentieth century would have been very different if the war had ended at that point. This essay contains the statement by Sir Kinglsey Wood, a cabinet minister in Britain during World War II who stated during a debate in the House of Commons on March 31, 1930, his recollection of being a participant in the Christmas Truce:

> "The fact is that we did it, and I then came to the conclusion that I have held very firmly ever since, that if we had been left by ourselves there would never have been another shot fired. For a fortnight the truce went on. We were on the most friendly terms, and it was only the fact that we were being controlled by others that made it necessary for us to start trying to shoot one

another again." He blamed the resumption of the war on "the grip of the political system which was bad, and I and others who were there at the time determined there and then never to rest . . . . Until we had seen whether we could change it." But they could not.

This book is not advocating either pacifism or isolationism. If a rogue nation launches an unprovoked attack then those attacked must defend themselves. But as is so often the case, history reveals the first shot was provoked by the other side and that the war was unnecessary and was promoted by certain insiders for hidden reasons. We have now reached the point in the nuclear age however, when we can no longer take the chance of going to war because our own leaders may have secretly provoked the attack, nor can we afford to go to war for reasons other than those which are just and for the defense of our own country. I believe that the survival of the human race may well depend upon developing a will to peace in the nuclear age. This book, hopefully, will contribute to creating that general will to peace by showing the benefits of true revisionism and how important it is to learn the lessons of history in order to prevent wars in the future.

1
A CENTURY OF WAR

THE MOST ACCURATE DESCRIPTION of the twentieth century is "The War and Welfare Century." This century was the bloodiest in all history. More than 170 million people were killed by governments with ten million being killed in World War I and fifty million killed in World War II. In regard to the fifty million killed in World War II, it is significant that nearly 70 percent were innocent civilians, mainly as a result of the bombing of cities by Great Britain and America.

This number of fifty million deaths does not include the estimated six to twelve million Russians killed by Stalin before World War II, and the several million people he killed after the war ended when Roosevelt delivered to him one-third of Europe as part of the settlement conferences. George Crocker's excellent book *Roosevelt's Road to Russia* describes the settlement conferences, such as Yalta, and shows how Roosevelt enhanced communism in Russia and China through deliberate concessions which strengthened it drastically, while Nazism was being extinguished in Germany.

It is inconceivable that America could join with Stalin as an ally and promote World War II as "the good war," against tyranny or totalitarianism. The war and American aid made Soviet Russia into a super military power which threatened America and the world for the next forty-five years. It delivered China to the communists and made it a threat during this same period of time.

The horror of the twentieth century could hardly have been predicted in the nineteenth century, which saw the eighteenth century end with the American Revolution bringing about the creation of the first classical liberal government. It was a government founded upon a blueprint in a written constitution, which allowed very few powers in the central government and protected individual liberties even from the vote of the majority. It provided for the ownership and protection of private property, free speech, freedom of religion, and basically a free-market economy with no direct taxes.

Both political factions united behind the first administration of President Washington to proclaim a foreign policy based upon noninterventionism and neutrality in the affairs of other nations, which remained the dominant political idea of America for over a hundred years.

These ideas of classical liberalism quickly spread to the Old World of Europe and at the end of the eighteenth century erupted into a different type of revolution in France, although a revolution in the name of liberty. The new ideal, however, adopted in the French Revolution was "equality" by force and it attempted to abolish all monarchy throughout Europe. The ideas of classical liberalism were twisted and distorted, but nevertheless were spread by force throughout Europe, thereby giving liberalism a bad name, especially in Germany; and this was accomplished by a conscripted French army.

The nineteenth century largely remained, in practice, a century of individual freedom, material progress, and relative peace, which allowed great developments in science, technology, and industry. However, the intellectual ferment toward the middle of the nineteenth century and thereafter was decidedly toward collectivism. In about 1850 the great classical liberal John Stuart Mill began to abandon these ideas and adopt socialism, as did most other intellectuals. After the brief Franco–Prussian War of 1870–71, Bismarck established the first welfare state while creating the nation of Germany by converting it from a confederation of states, just as Lincoln did in America. From this point up until World War I most German intellectuals began to glorify the state and collectivist ideas. They ignored one lone voice in Germany, a lyric poet by the name of Johann Christian Friedrich Hölderlin, who died in 1843. He stated, "What has made the State a hell on earth has been that man has tried to make it his heaven."[1] Hegel and Fichte immediately come to mind.

THE GREATEST TRAGEDY

Finally, the greatest tragedy of Western civilization erupted with World War I in 1914. It may be the most senseless, unnecessary and avoidable disaster in human history. Classical liberalism was thereby murdered, and virtually disappeared, and was replaced by collectivism which reigned both intellectually and in practice throughout the remainder of the twentieth century. The ideas of socialism began to take over the various governments of the world following World War I. Socialism was not initially a mass movement of the people but was a movement created by intellectuals who assumed important roles in the governments ruled by the collectivist politicians.

While I could quote from numerous political and intellectual leaders throughout the war and welfare century, I have chosen one who summed up the dominant political thoughts in the twentieth century. He was the founder of fascism, and he came to power in 1922 in Italy. In 1927 Benito Mussolini stated:

Fascism . . . believes neither in the possibility nor the utility of perpetual peace. . . . War alone brings up to its highest tension all human energy and puts the stamp of nobility upon the peoples who have the courage to meet it. . . . It may be expected that this will be a century of authority, a century of the Left, a century of Fascism. For the nineteenth century was a century of individualism. . . . [Liberalism always signifying individualism], it may be expected that this will be a century of collectivism, and hence the century of the State. . . . For Fascism, the growth of Empire, that is to say, the expansion of the nation, is the

---

[1]*The Collected Works of F.A. Hayek*, vol. 10: *Socialism and War: Essays, Documents, Reviews*, Bruce Caldwell, ed. (Chicago: University of Chicago Press, 1997), p. 175.

essential manifestation of vitality, and its opposite is a sign of decay and death.[2]

GUIDING PRINCIPLES

Mussolini's statement bears closer study because it dramatically states some of the guiding principles of the twentieth century:

1. It states that perpetual peace is neither possible, nor even to be desired.

2. Instead of peace, war is to be desired because not only is war a noble activity, but it reveals the true courage of man; it unleashes creative energy and causes progress. Moreover, war is the prime mover to enhance and glorify the state. War is the principal method by which collectivists have achieved their goal of control by the few over the many. They actually seek to create or initiate wars for this purpose.

3. Individualism, the philosophy practiced in the nineteenth century, is to be abolished and, specifically, collectivism is to rule the twentieth century.

4. Fascism is recognized as a variation of other forms of collectivism, all being part of the Left, as opposed to individualism. It was not until the "Red Decade" of the 30s, and the appearance of Hitler, that leftist intellectuals and the media began to switch Fascism on the political spectrum to the Right so that the "good forms of collectivism," such as socialism, could oppose the "extremism on the Right" which they said was fascism.

The founder of fascism clearly realized that all of these collectivist ideas, i.e., socialism, fascism and communism, belonged on the Left and were all opposed to individualism. Fascism is not an extreme form of individualism and is a part of the Left, or collectivism.

The ideals upon which America was founded were the exact opposite of those expressed by Mussolini and other collectivists on the Left. Why then was America, in the twentieth century, not a bulwark for freedom to oppose all of these leftist ideas?

---

[2]Benito Mussolini, "The Political and Social Doctrine of Fascism," in *Fascism: An Anthology*, Nathanael Greene, ed. (New York: Thomas Y. Crowell, 1968), pp. 41, 43–44.

Why didn't the ideas of the American Founders dominate the twentieth century and make it the "American Century of Peace and Prosperity" instead of the ideas of the Left dominating and making it the "War and Welfare Century"? The failure of the ideas of the Founders of America to be dominant in the twentieth century was certainly not because America had been conquered by the force of arms of some foreign leftist enemy.

The U.S. Empire

We need to learn the real reasons why America abandoned the principles of its Founding Fathers and allowed this tragedy to occur. We must determine why America became influenced by leftist thoughts, the ideas of empire, and the ideas of glorification of the state. How did America itself become an empire and an interventionist in World Wars I and II and help create the war and welfare century in which we now live?

We begin by examining a quotation from one of the main leaders of America in the nineteenth century and the answer becomes apparent. This statement was made in 1838 by a rather obscure American politician who would become world famous in 1861:

> At what point shall we expect the approach of danger? By what means shall we fortify against it? Shall we expect some transatlantic military giant, to step the Ocean, and crush us at a blow? Never! All the armies of Europe, Asia and Africa combined, with all the treasure of the earth . . . could not by force, take a drink from the Ohio, or make a track on the Blue Ridge, in a trial of a thousand years.[3]

Abraham Lincoln is the author of these words and he concluded his statement with the following:

> If destruction be our lot, we must ourselves be its author and finisher. As a nation of freemen, we must live through all time, or die by suicide.[4]

---

[3]The Collected Works of Abraham Lincoln, Roy P. Basler, ed. (New Brunswick, N.J.: Rutgers University Press, 1953–55), vol. 1, p. 109.

[4]Ibid.

Father Abraham

Abraham Lincoln himself became the principal instigator of America's suicide. It was not a foreign foe, but it was a war, a "victorious" war, that ended the Founders's dreams. However, many historians have never revealed the real cause and effect of the American Civil War, and instead have proclaimed it a "noble war" to free the slaves, and therefore, worth all of its costs. In fact, it was a war to repudiate the ideas of a limited central government and it moved America towards a domestic empire, which led inevitably to a foreign empire several decades later.

Photographs of Lincoln near the end of the war show signs of strain. However, I think the strain was due mainly to the fact that at the end of the long, bloody, and costly war, he understood that the war could have been avoided and that he had acted initially and primarily to secure the economic and political domination of the North over the South. Near the end of the war on February 3, 1865 a peace conference occurred on the presidential yacht at Hampton Roads, Virginia. Attending for the South were Vice President Alexander Stephens, John Campbell, a former U.S. Supreme Court Justice from Alabama, and a Mr. R.M.T. Hunter a member of the Confederate Senate. Attending for the North were President Lincoln and his Secretary of State, William Seward.[5]

It was agreed that no one else would be present and no transcription would be made but Alexander Stephens gives us all of the details. Lincoln stated he needed a commitment by the South to rejoin the Union. If the South made that initial commitment, the firing would stop and the South would be allowed to rejoin the Union with no punishment and their representatives would immediately return to Congress with the right to vote. William Seward pointed out that if the South accepted this proposal they could defeat, in Congress, the proposed 13th Amendment which was going to abolish slavery. Lincoln stated that the Emancipation Proclamation had been only a temporary war measure but that he felt that the Courts would allow approximately two hundred thousand (200,000) slaves already set free under that Proclamation to

---

[5]Alexander H. Stephens, *A Constitutional View of the War Between the States* (Harrisonburg, Va.: Sprinkle Publications, 1994), vol. 2, pp. 589–625.

remain free, but otherwise, slavery would remain in effect. Lincoln also stated that he felt that Congress would pass a bill to fully compensate the slave holders so that they could free their slaves. All three Southern delegates stated emphatically that they had no interest in trying to protect slavery and their only purpose in seceding was to gain independence from the central government in Washington. The conference thereupon ended.

Two key individuals recognized the real effect of the American Civil War. One of these was the great historian of liberty, Lord Acton, who wrote to a prominent American, Robert E. Lee, immediately after the war and stated:

> I saw in State Rights the only availing check upon the absolutism of the sovereign will, and secession filled me with hope, not as the destruction but as the redemption of Democracy. . . . Therefore, I deemed that you were fighting the battles of our liberty, our progress, and our civilization; and I mourn for the stake which was lost at Richmond more deeply than I rejoice over that which was saved at Waterloo.[6]

LEE'S VISION

With a careful analysis of the results of the Civil War, General Lee replied to Lord Acton in his letter dated December 15, 1866:

> I can only say that while I have considered the preservation of the constitutional power of the General Government to be the foundation of our peace and safety at home and abroad, I yet believe that the maintenance of the rights and authority reserved to the states and to the people, not only essential to the adjustment and balance of the general system, but the safeguard to the continuance of a free government. I consider it as the chief source of stability to our political system, whereas the consolidation of the states into one vast republic, sure to be *aggressive abroad* and *despotic at home*, will be the certain precursor of that ruin which has overwhelmed all those that have preceded it.[7]

---

[6]*Essays in the History of Liberty: Selected Writings of Lord Acton*, J. Rufus Fears, ed. (Indianapolis, Ind.: Liberty Classics, 1985), vol. 1, p. 277.

[7]Ibid., p. 364; emphasis added.

Lee clearly saw the North's victory as the beginning of the growth of empire, the loss of freedom to Americans and the destruction of the original ideas of our Founders. He also saw that the domestic empire would lead to an empire abroad. Consolidation of power into the central government is the basic premise of collectivism, and it was the basic idea the Constitution attempted to avoid. After the creation of the domestic American empire as a result of the Civil War, and then after the next three decades, America specifically repudiated its one-hundred-year old foreign policy and initiated the Spanish-American War, allegedly to free Cuba. We now know that the ultimate purpose of the war was to take the Philippine Islands from Spain in order to provide coaling stations for the trade with China which was considered by many American economic interests to be essential to America's expansion.

McKinley ordered the American warships sent to the Philippines at approximately the same time he sent the battleship *Maine* to Cuba and instructed the American Navy to support the Philippine rebels against their Spanish rulers. McKinley asked Congress to declare war because of the sinking of the battleship *Maine*, but we know today that the explosion occurred within the ship and, therefore, could not have been done by the Spanish. In the Philippines, the native rebels were successful in throwing off their Spanish rulers and were aided in their effort by the American Navy. Once the rebels had succeeded, McKinley ordered the American guns turned upon the rebels, murdering them in cold blood by the thousands, and snatched their islands away from them. McKinley then ruled as a military dictator without authority from Congress. Next, without any authority from Congress, he sent five thousand marines into China to help put down the Boxer Rebellion, which was an effort by the Chinese to expel foreigners from their own soil. McKinley joined with other European nations in seeking the spoils of China and sacrificed America's integrity and her right to be called a leader for freedom.

Next came the greatest tragedy of the twentieth century which was America's late entry into World War I. America's entry drastically changed the balance of power of the original contenders in the war and resulted in the horrible Treaty of Versailles, which paved the road to World War II.

The Progressive Movement

America's entry into World War I was a result of the so-called Progressive Movement which worshiped the idea of democracy *per se*, and wished to spread it throughout the world, by force if necessary. It was this movement which in one year, 1913, caused monumental changes in America, all in the name of attacking the rich for the benefit of the poor.

The first change was the creation of the Federal Reserve System allegedly to control the banks, but instead it concentrated power into the hands of an elite few unelected manipulators. The Sixteenth Amendment allowed for the income tax and it was alleged that the Amendment only attacked the rich. However, in World War I, the tax was raised and expanded and has become the most oppressive feature of American life in this century. Today it causes middle-class Americans to work approximately five months of every year just for the government before they earn anything for themselves.

The third drastic change was the Seventeenth Amendment which gave "power" to the people by letting them elect U.S. Senators rather than the state legislatures. The Founding Fathers had devised a system of state legislatures electing U.S. Senators in order to give the states the ability to restrain and limit the power of the federal government.

The Progressive Movement also promoted the personification of Isabel Paterson's "Humanitarian with a Guillotine," described in her book, *The God of the Machine*, by electing President Woodrow Wilson. He was a naive, idealistic, egomaniac, who took America into World War I. He did this to play a part in creating the League of Nations and help design the new structure of the world, thereby spreading the democratic gospel.

Wilson allowed the House of J.P. Morgan to become the exclusive agent for British purchases of war materials in America and further allowed Morgan to make loans and extend credit to the allies. Eventually, Wilson made the U.S. Government assume all of the Morgan debt and issued Liberty Bonds so the American taxpayers could help pay for it. When the allies refused to repay their debt, America stood on the precipice of an economic disaster, which was another major factor in Wilson's decision to enter the war. However, it was World War I and its destabilization of the economies of Western nations which led directly to the disaster of the Depression of 1929. There was no failure of the free market or the ideas of freedom which led to this economic disaster. It was caused by government interference in the market primarily resulting from World War I and the reaction of various governments to that war.

War Fever

As the war fever spread and the war drums beat, few people paid attention to such editorials as appeared in the *Commercial and Financial Journal* which stated:

> If war is declared, it is needless to say that we shall support the government. But may we not ask, one to another, before that fateful final word is spoken, are we not by this act transforming the glorious Republic that was, into the powerful Republic that is, and is to be? . . . Must we not admit that we are bringing into existence a new republic that is unlike the old?[8]

Wilson, like Polk, Lincoln, and McKinley before him, deceitfully made it appear that the alleged enemy started the war by firing the first shot. The German embassy warned Secretary of State Bryan that the British passenger ship, the *Lusitania*, was carrying illegal weapons and munitions, and was therefore a proper and perfectly legal target for submarines. Secretary of State William Jennings Bryan tried to get Wilson to warn Americans not to sail on this ship but he refused to do so, seeing that the opportunity for the loss of American lives would present him with an apparent reason for entering the war. Wilson failed to give the warning and Bryan later resigned. Over one hundred Americans were killed when a German submarine sank the *Lusitania*.

---

[8]Stuart D. Brandes, *Wardogs: A History of War Profits in America* (Lexington: University Press of Kentucky, 1997), p. 141.

VICTORY OVER FREEDOM

After World War I ended, President Wilson looked back to the harm he had brought on America and saw part of the true nature of World War I. In an address at St. Louis, Missouri on September 5, 1919, President Wilson stated:

> Why, my fellow-citizens, is there any man here, or any woman—let me say, is there any child here, who does not know that the seed of war in the modern world is industrial and commercial rivalry? . . . This war, in its inception, was a commercial and industrial war. It was not a political war.[9]

It is sad to contemplate the loss of liberty caused to Americans by the "victorious" wars we have fought when you look back and see that almost all of them were unnecessary to defend Americans or their freedom, and were largely economically instigated. In so many instances, the president provoked the other side into firing the first shot so it was made to appear that the war was started by America's alleged enemy. Not only did Polk, Lincoln, McKinley, and Wilson do this, but also later, Roosevelt would do it with Pearl Harbor and Johnson would do it at the Gulf of Tonkin for the Vietnam War.

It is not truly a study of history to speculate on what might have happened if America had not entered World War I, but here are some very reasonable, even probable, consequences if America had followed the advice of its Founders:

1. Almost certainly there would not have been a successful Bolshevik Revolution in Russia, giving communism a homeland from which to spread throughout the world.

2. A negotiated treaty between Germany and France and Great Britain, when all were wounded but undefeated, would have prevented the debacle of the Treaty of Versailles, the greatest single

---

[9]*The Papers of Woodrow Wilson*, Arthur S. Link, ed. (Princeton, N.J.: Princeton University Press, 1990), vol. 63, pp. 45–46.

tragedy of World War I. Without America's entry there would have been a treaty negotiated with co-equal partners, similar to the way the Congress of Vienna settled the Napoleonic Wars in 1815–16, with a defeated France still represented at the table by Tallyrand, and where a sincere effort was made to promote peace rather than cause a future war.

The Treaty of Versailles excluded Germany and Russia from the negotiations and declared Germany alone guilty of causing the war. It saddled her with tremendous payments for war damages and took away much of her territory. The Treaty of Versailles paved the way for Hitler whose support came democratically from the German people who wanted to throw off the unfair Treaty. Without the rise of communism in Russia and Nazism in Germany, World War II probably would not have occurred.

The Habsburg Monarchy

I want to add a footnote here relative to the settlement of World War I as it relates to the Habsburg Monarchy. In his excellent book entitled *Leftism Revisited*, Erik von Kuehnelt-Leddihn reveals that President Wilson probably was unaware of the wisdom of Disraeli's words: "The maintenance of the Austrian Empire is necessary to the independence and, if necessary, to the civilization and even to the liberties of Europe." The book points out that President Wilson had as one of his main foreign-policy representatives a confirmed socialist preacher by the name of Reverend George Davis Herron.

The Habsburg Monarchy petitioned Wilson to negotiate a separate peace treaty in February of 1918, before the war ended later in November and sent as its representative Professor Heinrich Lammasch to meet with the American representative Reverend Herron. They spent two days together and Professor Lammasch revealed the plan to create a federated political body which was entirely in keeping with one of Wilson's Fourteen Points; i.e., that individual nations (ethnic groups) would be "accorded the freest opportunity of autonomous development." The book states:

During the night he [Herron] began to wrestle with this "temptation," as "Jacob wrestled with God near the Yabbok." By morning he knew that he had gained complete victory over himself; Lammasch had been nothing but an evil tempter. No! The Habsburg Monarchy had to go because the Habsburgs as such were an obstacle to progress, democracy, and liberty. Had they remained in power the whole war would have been fought in vain.[10]

Of course, one of the winners of the war, Great Britain, was allowed to keep its monarchy.

Bolsheviks and the Kingdom of Heaven

The book continues with an interesting event relating to Reverend Herron after his travels in Europe. He wrote to the socialist, Norman Thomas, in 1920 and stated that: The "Bolsheviks" were bad, but the "future civilization of Europe is coming out of Russia and it will be at least an approach to the Kingdom of Heaven when it comes."[11] The leftist bias and bent of mind of Wilson's representative is crystal clear and communism is proclaimed to be the great political system of the future.

There are many important lessons that the twentieth century, this "War and Welfare Century," should teach us. One of these is summed up by Bruce Porter in his excellent book entitled *War and the Rise of the State* wherein he states that the New Deal "was the only time in U.S. history when the power of the central state grew substantially in the absence of war."[12] He concluded that:

Throughout the history of the United States, war has been the primary impetus behind the growth and development of the central state. It has been the lever by which presidents and other national officials have bolstered the power of the state in

---

[10]Erik von Kuehnelt-Leddihn, *LeftismRevisited: From de Sade and Marx to Hitler and Pol Pot* (Washington, D.C.: Regnery Gateway, 1990), p. 214.

[11]Ibid., p. 216.

[12]Bruce D. Porter, *War and the Rise of the State: The Military Foundations of Modern Politics* (New York: Free Press, 1994), p. 278.

the face of tenacious popular resistance. It has been a wellspring of American nationalism and a spur to political and social change.[13]

The same lesson is contained in a warning issued by the great champion of liberty and student of American democracy, Alexis de Tocqueville, who warned America in the early part of the nineteenth century that:

> No protracted war can fail to endanger the freedom of a democratic country. . . . War does not always give over democratic communities to military government, but it must invariably and immeasurably increase the powers of civil government; it must almost compulsorily concentrate the direction of all men and the management of all things in the hands of the administration. If it does not lead to despotism by sudden violence, it prepares men for it more gently by their habits. All those who seek to destroy the liberties of a democratic nation ought to know that war is the surest and the shortest means to accomplish it. This is the first axiom of the science.[14]

Both Porter and Tocqueville are warning us that even "victorious" wars cause the loss of freedom due to the centralization of power into the federal government. Another lesson is that democracy *per se* will not protect our freedom or individual liberty. I have heard college students ask the question: "Why did the Greeks, who invented democracy, remain so critical of it?" The answer, of course, is that democracy, without proper restraints and limitation of powers as provided in the original American Constitution, can be just as tyrannical as a single despot. F.A. Hayek made this point when he stated:

> There can be no doubt that in history there has often been much more cultural and political freedom under an autocratic rule than under some democracies—and it is at least conceivable

---

[13]Ibid., p. 291.

[14]Alexis de Tocqueville, *Democracy in America* (New York: Alfred A. Knopf, 1980), vol. 2, pp. 268–69.

that under the government of a very homogeneous doctrinaire majority, democratic government might be as oppressive as the worst dictatorship.[15]

Limiting the State

We should learn from the war and welfare century that the greatest discovery in Western civilization was that liberty could be achieved only through the proper and effective limitation on the power of the state. It is this limitation on the power of the state which protects private property, a free-market economy, personal liberties and promotes a noninterventionist foreign policy, which, if coupled with a strong *national* defense, will bring peace and prosperity instead of war and welfare. It is not democracy *per se* which protects freedom.

Too many people living in democracies are lulled into believing that they are free because they have the right to vote and elections are held periodically. If you take conscription for military service as an example, I think you would find that if it was proclaimed by a sole monarch, the people would revolt and disobey. However, in a democracy, when the politicians vote for it, the people comply and still think they are free.

The fall of the Berlin wall and the demise of the Soviet Empire do not assure us that collectivism is dead. I predict that the next assault on freedom by the new leftist intellectuals will be through the democratic process, maybe coupled with a religious movement, but certainly not coupled with antireligious ideas. Many, maybe most Americans, who opposed Communist Russia, were convinced it was wrong and evil because it was atheistic and not because its political and economic ideas were wrong and evil. I think the new collectivist monster will be dressed in different clothing advocating equality, justice, democracy, religion, and market socialism.

---

[15]*The Collected Works of F.A. Hayek*, Caldwell, ed., p. 209.

Intellectuals of the Future

It will then be more important than ever for intellectuals of the future to have a correct understanding of the philosophy of individual freedom and of free-market economics in order to fight collectivism in the twenty-first century. It will be most important for Americans to understand why Ludwig von Mises, in his book, *Omnipotent Government*, stated:

> Durable peace is only possible under perfect capitalism, hitherto never and nowhere completely tried or achieved. In such a Jeffersonian world of the unhampered market economy the scope of government activities is limited to the protection of lives, health, and property of individuals against violence or fraudulent aggression.[16]
>
> All the oratory of the advocates of government omnipotence cannot annul the fact there is but one system that makes for durable peace: a free-market economy. Government control leads to economic nationalism and thus results in conflict.[17]

The definition of a free market, which Mises states will allow us to have peace and prosperity, is one where the economy is not only free of government control, but also where economic interests do not control the government policy, especially foreign policy, which has been the case throughout the twentieth century and continues to the present time. The highest risk for war is where various economic interests are able to control foreign policy to promote their particular interests rather than the well-being and liberty of the individuals within a society.

---

[16]Ludwig von Mises, *Omnipotent Government: The Rise of the Total State and Total War* (New Rochelle, N.Y.: Arlington House, 1969), p. 284.

[17]Ibid., p. 286.

2

ABRAHAM LINCOLN AND

THE FIRST SHOT

IN ALMOST EVERY POLL of public opinion or assessment by professional historians which has been published since World War II, Presidents Abraham Lincoln and Franklin Roosevelt rank in the top three as two of our "greatest."[1] Arthur M. Schlesinger, Sr., who conducted the first poll of historians in 1948, concluded that the ratings as to "greatness" were heavily influenced by a particular president's connection with "some turning point in our history."[2] Undoubtedly, the American Civil War and World War II were major "turning points" in American history and therefore greatly influenced the high ratings of these two presidents. The position of "greatness," however, necessarily assumes that neither of these presidents had any guilt in bringing on these wars. Instead, it is assumed that both presidents were peace-seekers, trying to lead the nation toward a reconciliation of its problems and trying to avoid a war until the enemy fired the first shot and forced an unwanted war upon these presidents and the American people.

The Roman lawyer Cicero struggled with the question of what is a "just war," as did the Christian philosophers of the Medieval

---

[1]Robert Murray and Tim H. Blessing, "The Presidential Performance Study: A Progress Report," *Journal of American History* 70 (December 1983): 535.

[2]Ibid., p. 553.

period, from Augustine to Aquinas. Later, the father of international law, the Dutchman Hugo Grotius, addressed the question also because he was concerned that wars which Christians might fight would be done with a clear conscience toward God. As a result of these developing ideas, Western political leaders have tried to convince their citizens or subjects that their wars met one of the main criteria; that is, that the wars were "defensive." President John F. Kennedy declared in January 1961 that "Our arms will never be used to strike the first blow in any attack. . . . It is our national tradition."[3] It has always been important to American presidents to try to demonstrate that the enemy fired the first shot and started the war.

Those who support the mythology that surrounds Lincoln and Franklin Roosevelt have tried to resist the nagging question which continues to assert itself about whether these presidents actually maneuvered the enemy into firing the first shot in order to produce wars that they wanted but that the people did not. In both cases, war caused great power and prestige to flow to the presidency, and most of the imagined "greatness" of these two presidents therefore arises from their perceived conduct as war leaders and protectors of "American liberty and rights." I will first address the question concerning the Lincoln administration and in a subsequent chapter will examine President Franklin Roosevelt. Nonetheless, the question in regard to both is whether they provoked the enemy into firing the first shot.

Most wars are fought for economic reasons, but the general population will rarely rally around the flag for such causes; therefore, other reasons are usually given for the purpose of any war, in order to persuade mothers and fathers to send their sons off to an uncertain future which could very easily result in their return in body bags. For this reason, both the Civil War and World War II have been clothed in a mythology which states that the Civil War was fought for the purpose of "abolishing slavery" and World War II was fought to oppose "tyranny" or "Fascism."

---

[3]Richard N. Current, *Lincoln and The First Shot* (Prospect Heights, Ill.: Waveland Press, 1963), p. 7.

The investigation of why the South fired the first shot at Fort Sumter raises the question of whether the firing on Fort Sumter by the South started the war or whether there were preceding, provocative, and precipitating acts on the part of President Lincoln and his administration which caused the South to fire first.

One of the essential reasons the South wanted out of the Union was to avoid economic exploitation by the North, and one of the main reasons the Northern political and economic interests refused to allow the South to secede was that they wanted to continue this economic exploitation. The long-standing dispute over slavery that existed between the North and South was not whether slavery should be abolished where it already existed but, rather, whether slavery should be expanded into the new territories and new states. The small but vociferous band of abolitionists in the North were the only ones calling for the abolition of slavery where it already existed and this could have been accomplished through the secession of the North. The abolitionists argued that secession would relieve the North from the obligation to enforce the fugitive slave clause in the Constitution, which required the North to return slaves. Both Horace Greely, owner of the *New York Tribune*, and the abolitionist Harry Ward Beecher said, "Let the South go."[4] The abolitionists, however, were very unpopular in the North, primarily because secession was not a popular issue there just before the Civil War, although it had been in previous times.[5] The concern of the North was that if slavery was expanded into new states, the South would have more representation in Congress in both the House and Senate, thereby allowing the South to protect itself from economic exploitation.

---

[4]W.A. Swanberg, *First Blood: The Story of Fort Sumter* (New York: Charles Scribener's Sons, 1957), p. 155.

[5]See David Gordon, ed., *Secession, State and Liberty* (New Brunswick, N.J.: Transaction Publishers, 1998), which covers the subject of secession in America thoroughly and shows that both the North and the South had championed this "right" and both had threatened to secede on numerous occasions before the Civil War.

The story of the cause of the Civil War goes all the way back to the Constitutional Convention in which one of the major dis-putes was whether a simple majority vote or a two-thirds vote would be required for the passage of the Navigation Acts, which included the tariff legislation. Both at the time of the adoption of the Constitution and the Civil War, the tariff constituted the pri-mary revenue (more than 80 percent) for the federal government. George Mason, one of the Virginia delegates to the Constitutional Convention, argued for a two-thirds vote as follows:

> If the Government is to be lasting, it must be founded in the confidence and affections of the people, and must be so con-structed as to obtain these. The *Majority* will be governed by their interests. The Southern States are the *minority* in both Houses. Is it to be expected that they will deliver themselves bound hand & foot to the Eastern States, and enable them to exclaim, in the words of Cromwell on a certain occasion—"the lord hath delivered them into our hands."[6]

Fellow Virginia delegate James Madison, who was a strong supporter of the Constitution and, in fact, is known to us today as "The Father of the Constitution," resisted Mason's request for a two-thirds vote and argued that there would be no exploitation of the South if there was a simple majority vote to enact tariff leg-islation.[7] The final draft of the Constitution that was approved in Philadelphia had only a simple majority requirement for tariff leg-islation, and Mason refused to sign the document. One writer, in analyzing this dispute over the tariff between Mason and Madi-son—which later became the most important cause of the Amer-ican Civil War—shows that Mason continued his opposition to

---

[6]Gaillard Hunt and James Brown Scott, eds., *The Debates in the Federal Convention of 1787 Which Framed the Constitution of the United States of America* (Buffalo, N.Y.: Prometheus Books, 1987), vol. 2, p. 485. Also see p. 575 for Mason's statement about the two-thirds vote and p. 582 for his refusal to sign the Constitution along with Randolph and Gerry.

[7]Ibid., p. 485.

the Constitution in the Virginia ratification convention by continuing to demand a two-thirds vote on any tariff legislation.[8]

At the time of the adoption of the Constitution, the North had a larger population than the South, but there was an attempt to compensate for this by counting a fraction of the slave population as part of the total population for determining representation in the House of Representatives—a concept that became known as the "federal ratio." One of the reasons the Northern politicians opposed slavery was that it gave the South too much political power. Another factor was that the North quickly adapted to the Industrial Revolution which had started in England and then crossed the Atlantic, causing the North to become more industrial than agricultural by 1820. The new industrial jobs caused a rapid increase in the population of the North, which gave it much more representation in the House of Representatives, but this factor was partially balanced by the practice of admitting two new states at a time with one being a slave state and the other being a free state so that representation in the Senate remained equal. The South also sought to protect itself by sending its most prominent citizens to Congress and by a close cooperation with Northern Democrats.

---

[8]See K.R. Constantine Gutzman, "'Oh, What a Tangled Web We Weave . . .': James Madison and the Compound Republic," *Continuity: A Journal of History* 22 (1998): 24.

> In our own day, with the NAFTA and GATT controversies, we have been reminded of the potentially contentious nature of trade arguments. In Madison's day, such disputes were even more contentious, even more acrimonious. Especially after Henry Clay's "American System" speech of 1824, in which the Kentuckian frankly admitted that his program was an intersectional transfer of wealth, tariff arguments were potentially violent. Mason predicted in Philadelphia that the requirement of a bare majority for the enactment of tariff legislation would lead to Northern exploitation of the South of the kind Clay later made famous. Madison immediately issued a long declamation on the impossibility of such a turn of events.

In 1824, Kentuckian Henry Clay made his famous "American System" speech and frankly admitted that the tariff should be high enough to protect "American" industry from manufactured imports from Europe, primarily England. A tariff levied on an import could be made high enough that a purchaser would be better off buying the Northern-made product. As the South was almost entirely an agricultural region, it had to buy almost all of its manufactured products either from Europe, and pay the protective tariff, or from Northern industries, and pay, in most cases, an excessive price. About three-fourths of the total tariff collected in the U.S. was paid by the Southerners. Another development which began to divide the North and South was that the political power of the North also allowed it to keep a vast majority of the tariff revenue and use it for "internal improvements," such as building harbors and canals, which was, in effect, a corporate welfare program. The North claimed a right to do this under the "general welfare" clause of the Constitution, but the South objected, stating that this was an incorrect understanding of the meaning of this clause. Internal improvements were also a major part of Henry Clay's "American System," which in reality was a partnership between government and the business interests in the North.

In 1828, the North had enough political power to pass an extremely high protective tariff, which became known as the "Tariff of Abominations." This led to the nullification movement in South Carolina in 1832 under the leadership of John C. Calhoun. South Carolina declared that the tariff was nullified or void in the state of South Carolina; however, a subsequent reduction in the tariff by Congress settled the problem temporarily. Charleston, South Carolina, was the primary focus of this entire battle because this was where most of the tariff was collected, and Fort Sumter, manned by federal troops, constituted the means for enforcement of the collection of the tariff. The tariff continued to be an extremely hot issue between the North and South up to the Civil War, with Henry Clay being both an instigator and pacificator of the conflict until his death in 1852.[9]

---

[9]For a full discussion of the tariff issue, see three books by Charles Adams, *For Good and Evil: The Impact of Taxes on the Course of Civilization,*

The new Republican Party, which had only come into existence in 1854, adopted a platform in 1860 that explicitly called for a high protective tariff and internal improvements and, therefore, was a direct threat to the South. Lincoln fully subscribed to this platform before and after his presidential nomination by the Republicans. Lincoln won his election with less than 40 percent of the popular vote, carrying only eighteen of thirty-three states, and he did not have a single electoral vote cast for him in the South. While Lincoln's position on the tariff and internal improvements was an ominous economic sign, the South still had hope that Lincoln would not oppose secession. During Lincoln's one term in Congress, he had been a vocal opponent of the Mexican War of 1846 and had supported the right of secession as a way of protesting the war. The threat of secession had been asserted, not only by the South because of the tariff, but by the North, especially New England, on numerous occasions: in 1803 with the Louisiana Purchase, at the Hartford Convention in opposition to the War of 1812, and then again, at the time of the Mexican War.[10] Lincoln proclaimed his strong endorsement of the right of secession in 1847 as follows:

> Any people, anywhere, being inclined and having the power, have the right to rise up and shake off the existing government,

---

2nd ed. (New York: Madison Books, 1999), pp. 329–43, *Those Dirty Rotten Taxes: The Tax Revolts that Built America* (New York: The Free Press, 1998), pp. 81–112, and *When In The Course of Human Events: Arguing the Case for Southern Secession* (Lanham, Md.: Rowman & Littlefield, 2000). See also Kenneth M. Stampp, *And the War Came: The North and the Secession Crisis, 1860–1861* (Baton Rouge: Louisiana State University Press, 1990), pp. 2, 4, 43–44, 161–64, 231–38. Finally, see Phillip S. Foner, *Business and Slavery: The New York Merchants and The Irrepressible Conflict* (Chapel Hill, N.C.: Duke University Press. 1941), pp. 275–305.

[10]For a full discussion, see Donald W. Livingston, "The Secession Tradition in America," pp. 1–33, and Thomas J. DiLorenzo, "Yankee Confederates: New England Secessionists Movement Prior to the War Between the States," pp. 135–53, in David Gordon, ed., *Secession, State and Liberty* (New Brunswick, N.J.: Transaction Publishers, 1998).

and form a new one that suits them better. *This is a most valuable, a most sacred right, a right which we hope and believe is to liberate the world.*[11]

After the election of 1860, the new Republican Party was very much a minority in both the House and Senate, and it claimed only one Supreme Court justice. This new political party was made up of some abolitionists and former Democrats, but mostly former Whigs like Lincoln, who stood for a strong centralized government, a high protective tariff, internal improvements, a loose interpretation of the Constitution, and a partnership between big business in the North and government that would allow business to expand westward, and even to other countries, if necessary.

As soon as Lincoln was elected, attention again focused on South Carolina because of the tariff issue. There were three federal forts in the Charleston harbor, but Fort Sumter stood squarely in the middle of the channel and constituted the main weapon for enforcement of the tariff. Should South Carolina secede, it would be imperative to reclaim the fort. At the time of South Carolina's coming into the Union, it had made a gift or deed of trust of the land and Fort Sumter to the federal government. Because the fort also provided the ultimate defense from invasion of the harbor, whoever controlled Fort Sumter would control Charleston, a key Southern city.

On December 9, 1860, all the congressmen from South Carolina met with President Buchanan in Washington and got a verbal pledge from him that he would not make any move to reinforce Fort Sumter.[12] Unknown to the South, President-elect Lincoln, who would not take office until March 4, 1861, communicated directly on December 12, 1860, with General Winfield Scott, head of the army under the Buchanan administration, and told him to be sure to hold and retake all federal forts in the

---

[11]John Shipley Tilley, *Lincoln Takes Command* (Nashville, Tenn.: Bill Coats, 1991), p. xv; emphasis added.

[12]Ibid., p. 121.

South.[13] Soon thereafter, on December 20, South Carolina became the first state to leave the Union. Six days later, Major Anderson, on his own initiative, moved his federal troops into Fort Sumter from Fort Moultrie, a nearby military installation. There was an immediate uproar throughout the South, and Senator Jefferson Davis of Mississippi asserted that this was an overt act of war on the part of President Buchanan, who indicated truthfully that he had not authorized this reinforcement of Fort Sumter.[14] Governor Pickens of South Carolina complained to President Buchanan and again received assurances from him that there would not be any further reinforcement of any forts in South Carolina, and especially Fort Sumter.[15]

Major Anderson wrote a letter to his commanding officer in Washington on December 26, 1860, reporting that he had one year's supply of hospital stores as well as food provisions for about four months, which would be through April 26, 1861.[16] This food supply was that which was available in Fort Sumter, but Anderson quickly developed a good relationship with the mayor of Charleston and other local Charleston merchants, so that from that point on, he was getting daily supplies from grocers and butchers. Therefore, Anderson was in no danger of lack of food supplies from this point up until just a few days before the firing on Fort Sumter. Also, following Anderson's move to Fort Sumter, Secretary of War Floyd resigned, stating that Anderson's action was an act of bad faith on the part of the Buchanan administration which he could no longer support.[17]

Before continuing with the full story of Fort Sumter, it is important to look at the other key fort that was a focal point of dispute between the North and South at this time—that is, Fort Pickens in Pensacola Bay, Florida—because this also sheds light upon Lincoln's intentions and actions at Fort Sumter. While Fort

---

[13]Ibid., pp. 105–06.

[14]Ibid., p. 110.

[15]Ibid., p. 122.

[16]Ibid.

[17]Ibid., p. 126.

Pickens was not a primary tariff collection port, it was an essential military installation for the Southern part of the United States and for the Confederacy. The state of Florida seceded from the Union on January 10, 1861, and through its former U.S. senator, Stephen Mallory, and its governor, made an immediate demand upon President Buchanan on January 15, for the return of Fort Pickens and the immediate evacuation of all federal troops. After much discussion and threats from both sides, the state of Florida and the Buchanan administration entered into a formal truce on January 29. The agreement was that if there was no reinforcement of Fort Pickens by the North, then the South would not fire upon the fort, which would allow time for the parties to attempt to work out their other differences.

After Lincoln's inauguration on March 4, 1861, he violated this truce by issuing secret executive orders on March 11 and 12 to send reinforcements to Fort Pickens. The order was actually signed by General Winfield Scott, who kept the same position in the Lincoln administration as he had in the previous administration as head of the army. When Captain Adams of the U.S. Navy, who was in charge of Fort Pickens, received the order from General Scott in March 1861 to send out boats to pick up reinforcements on the warships that were near the harbor, Adams refused to obey the order. Adams was very familiar with the terms of the truce and thought there had been some misunderstanding by the new administration. He knew this reinforcement was an explicit violation of the agreement without any provocation on the part of the South. He fully realized that this act alone would start the war. Furthermore, as a captain in the navy, he was unwilling to take an order from General Scott, who was head of the army, so he sent word back that he wanted clarification from his naval commander.[18]

On April 1, President Lincoln issued a series of secret executive orders, some over his name and some over the name of Secretary of the Navy Gideon Wells, to send troops to reinforce Fort

---

[18]Ibid., pp. 48–52.

Pickens. Captain M.C. Meigs was present in the office of the president when he issued these orders, and Meigs wrote a letter dated April 6, in which he explained his reaction to the events he had observed on April 1.

> While the mere throwing of a few men into Fort Pickens may seem a small operation, the opening of the campaign is a great one. Unless this movement is followed up by the navy and supported by ample supplies . . . it will be a failure. This is the beginning of the war.[19]

Captain Meigs clearly saw that the act of reinforcement was an act of war and violated the truce that existed between the United States and Florida (and the Confederacy), and that war was being started secretly by the act of the president without any consultation with Congress. The warships came to Pensacola harbor, but because reinforcement actually did not take place until the night of April 12 under the complete cover of darkness, it was not perceived by the South until the next day.[20] Negotiations continued, however, after the South discovered the violation of the truce, and the military commanders were still exchanging communications until April 17, before any shots were fired.[21]

Later, after the war had started and Lincoln had addressed Congress on July 4, 1861, Congress made a written inquiry dated July 19, requesting documents about the armistice at Fort Pickens. President Lincoln replied by sending Navy Secretary Wells to Congress with a written message dated July 30, in which the president declined to produce any documents, claiming executive privilege, and stating "it is believed the communication of the information called for would not, at this time, comport with the public interest."[22]

---

[19]Ibid., p. 63.

[20]Ibid., p. 66.

[21]Ibid., p. 75.

[22]Ibid., p. 92.

Returning now to the developments at Fort Sumter, a major event occurred there on January 9, 1861. Without prior notice to or knowledge of Major Anderson at Fort Sumter, a merchant ship named *Star of the West* entered Charleston harbor and headed toward Fort Sumter. It had been learned by the South, just prior to this event, that hidden below the deck were two hundred armed soldiers with ammunition, and supplies; therefore, the South Carolina troops fired a shot across the bow as a warning to the ship, which then reversed its course and left the area. Secretary of Interior Thompson resigned his position in the Buchanan administration over this incident, saying that it indicated bad faith on the part of the administration.[23] President Buchanan again claimed that the event occurred without his authority, but actually he had authorized the attempt to reinforce and then unsuccessfully tried to revoke the order.[24] On January 12, Governor Pickens of South Carolina again demanded the return of the fort, but President Buchanan stated he had no authority to do so.[25] Even though the fort had been a gift from South Carolina to the Union, South Carolina was willing to pay fair-market value for all of the land and improvements in exchange for its return and the evacuation of the federal troops. Governor Pickens at this time made it clear to President Buchanan and his administration, a position which soon became public knowledge, that any future attempt by any ship to provide reinforcements would immediately cause South Carolina to fire directly upon the ship and Fort Sumter.[26] Also in the discussions with President Buchanan, it was pointed out that simply the act of sending the ship for reinforcement was an act of war and would not be tolerated.[27]

---

[23]Ibid., p. 156.

[24]Swanberg, *First Blood: The Story of Fort Sumter*, pp. 121, 123, 127, 145.

[25]Tilley, *Lincoln Takes Command*, pp. 149–51.

[26]Ibid., p. 152.

[27]Ibid.

On February 4, the Confederate government had taken over jurisdiction of all federal property still located in the South, which included both Forts Sumter and Pickens.[28] On February 6, President Buchanan also reaffirmed the armistice in regard to Fort Pickens to the effect that there would be no further reinforcements. As he had earlier indicated, this was also the case at Fort Sumter. In return, the South would not fire on either fort as long as no reinforcement was attempted.

On February 7, retired Navy Captain Gustavus Fox approached the Buchanan administration and General Winfield Scott, in particular, with his secret plan to reinforce Fort Sumter successfully. It called for a nighttime maneuver involving several tugs to go first, pulling whaling boats full of men and supplies, and then several warships with more troops to follow. General Scott presented Fox and his plan to Secretary of War Holt, who liked the plan, but on the next day Scott informed Fox that any plans to reinforce Fort Sumter were being abandoned by the Buchanan administration.[29]

On March 2, President Buchanan signed the Morrill Tariff into law, which was the highest protective tariff in American history, and by early 1862, it reached the average amount of 47.06 percent.[30] The Morrill Tariff remained the cornerstone policy of the Republican Party up through the twentieth century. President Buchanan was from Pennsylvania, a traditional high-tariff state, and even though he was leaving office in two days, he wanted to protect his political career by signing this act, which was popular in Pennsylvania but an ominous threat to the South. Two days later, on March 4, the nation waited with great anticipation for President Lincoln's Inaugural Address. Lincoln addressed the question of slavery directly and openly by quoting from one of his previously published speeches:

---

[28]Ibid., p. 154.

[29]Ibid., p. 153.

[30]Frank Taussig, *The Tariff History of the United States* (New York: Putnam, 1931), p. 167.

I have no purpose, directly or indirectly, to interfere with the institution of slavery in the States where it exists. I believe I have no lawful right to do so, and I have no inclination to do so.[31]

Lincoln had also required each of his cabinet members to take a solemn pledge that they would enforce the Constitution, and particularly the fugitive slave clause, which required the North to return fugitive slaves to the South.[32] Lincoln specifically promised in his speech to enforce this clause. Furthermore, historian David Potter points out that:

> Lincoln returned, later in his speech, to the question of Constitutional protection for slavery in the states. He alluded to the proposed Thirteenth Amendment, just passed by Congress, to guarantee slavery in the states, and added that, although he wished to speak of general policy, rather than specific measures, he would say that, holding such a guarantee to be implied in the existing Constitution, "I have no objection to its being made express and irrevocable."[33]

President Lincoln thereby completely removed the slavery issue from contention between the North and South by promising to enforce the fugitive slave clause and supporting a Constitutional amendment which would explicitly protect slavery. The protection for slavery had only been implied in the original Constitution in three places; that is, the fugitive slave clause, the ban on the slave trade, and the three-fifths ratio clause.

Lincoln apologists often point to the following concluding gesture to the South in the Inaugural Address to prove that he wanted peace instead of war:

---

[31]David M. Potter, *Lincoln and His Party in the Secession Crisis* (Baton Rouge: Louisiana State University Press, 1995), p. 321.

[32]John Nevin, *Gideon Welles, Lincoln's Secretary of Navy* (Baton Rouge: Louisiana State University Press, 1994), p. 311.

[33]Potter, *Lincoln and His Party in the Secession Crisis*, p. 321.

In your hands, my dissatisfied fellow countrymen, and not in mine, is the momentous issue of civil war. The government will not assail you. You can have no conflict without being your-selves the aggressors.[34]

The mythology which has surrounded Lincoln usually cites the above quotation as showing that Lincoln was doing every-thing within his power to prevent a war. However, immediately after his Inaugural Address, the South considered the speech to have been a declaration of war by Lincoln, even though Lincoln said nothing that threatened the institution of slavery in the South. Therefore, there must have been other words in his address which caused the South to consider that he had declared war. We find those words in his speech:

The power confided to me will be used to hold, occupy, and possess the property and places belonging to the government, *and to collect the duties and imposts*; but beyond what *may be nec-essary for these objects*, there will be no *invasion*, no *using of force* against or among the people anywhere.[35]

Senator Wigfall of Texas immediately notified Governor Pick-ens that the address meant war sooner or later, and in all likeli-hood, no time should be lost in sending reinforcements to Fort Sumter.[36] Another prominent Southerner, L.Q. Washington, who was in Washington, D.C., and heard the address, forwarded to Confederate Secretary of War Leroy Walker a letter echoing Wig-fall's opinion, which undoubtedly was shared with the members of the Confederate cabinet. The letter stated:

We all put the same construction on the inaugural, which we carefully went over together. We agreed that it was *Lincoln's*

---

[34]Charles W. Ramsdell, "Lincoln and Fort Sumter," *The Journal of Southern History* 3 (Southern Historical Association, February–November, 1937): 264.

[35]Carl Van Doren, ed., "First Inaugural Address," *The Literary Works of Abraham Lincoln* (Norwalk, Conn.: Easton Press, 1970), pp. 177–78; emphasis added.

[36]Tilley, *Lincoln Takes Command*, p. 163.

purpose at once to attempt the collection of the revenue, to re-enforce and hold Forts Sumter and Pickens, and to retake the other places.

We believe that these plans will be put into execution immediately. I learned five or six United States ships are in New York Harbor, all ready to start. The United States steamer *Pawnee* came here the other day suddenly from Philadelphia, fully provisioned and ready to go to sea.[37]

Furthermore, President Lincoln, in his Inaugural Address, repudiated his prior stand taken during the Mexican War that secession was a "most valuable, a most sacred right" of each state within the Union and proclaimed that "no state upon its own mere motion, can lawfully get out of the Union."[38] Later, during the war, however, Lincoln again recognized the right of forty-nine counties to secede from Virginia and to become the new state of West Virginia. The creation of the new state in this manner violated Article V, Section 3, of the Constitution, but nevertheless took place solely because of the pledge of loyalty of the residents of West Virginia. Of course, this added two new senators and additional representatives, who were all loyal to Lincoln.

In accordance with the resolution of the Confederate Congress, President Davis appointed three commissioners to negotiate with the United States all questions of disagreement between the two governments.[39] The appointments took place on February 25, and reached Washington on March 5, the day after Lincoln's inauguration. The Confederate government was offering to assume its proportion of any federal debt and pay fair market value for all federal property remaining within the seceding states. It also sought recognition of its independence as a separate government by the Lincoln administration. Davis had stated that the South simply wanted to be let alone and constituted no threat to the existing government in Washington: "We seek no conquest,

---

[37]Ibid., pp. 163–64; emphasis added.

[38]Potter, *Lincoln and His Party in the Secession Crisis*, p. 322.

[39]Ramsdell, "Lincoln and Fort Sumter," p. 264.

no aggrandizement, no concession of any kind . . . all we ask is to be let alone."[40]

President Lincoln refused to see the commissioners, refused to negotiate any peace terms, and, furthermore, refused to recognize the Confederate government. In regard to Fort Sumter, he continued to deal only with Governor Pickens of South Carolina. The commissioners were never able to speak directly with President Lincoln; and, as will be shown in more detail later, their negotiations had to go through two U.S. Supreme Court justices to Secretary of State Seward, who led them to believe that he spoke for the Lincoln administration.

Meanwhile, on March 9, President Lincoln asked his primary military advisor, General Winfield Scott, to investigate Major Anderson's condition at Fort Sumter and advise him on the feasibility of reinforcement. The diary of Attorney General Edward Bates reveals that a cabinet meeting was held on March 9 to consider the desirability of sending reinforcements to Charleston. The army and navy military representatives presented their opinions, which were recorded by Bates with the following language in his diary: "The naval men have convinced me fully that the thing can be done, *and yet as the doing of it would be almost certain to begin the war* . . . I am willing to yield to the military counsel and evacuate Fort Sumter."[41] However, on March 11, as we have already seen, President Lincoln told General Scott to issue an order to reinforce Fort Pickens, which order was refused by Captain Adams. Also, on March 11, Senator Wigfall of Texas telegraphed General Beauregard stating that the opinion in Washington was that there had been a cabinet meeting, and it had been decided that Anderson would be ordered to evacuate Fort Sumter within five days.[42] On March 12, Postmaster General Blair contacted his brother-in-law, retired naval officer Gustavus Fox, and took him personally to see President Lincoln in order to explain his reinforcement plan

---

[40]William C. Davis, *A Government of Our Own: The Making of the Confederacy* (New York: The Free Press, 1994), pp. 340–41.

[41]Tilley, *Lincoln Takes Command*, p. 165; emphasis added.

[42]Ibid.

which had been rejected by the Buchanan administration.[43] After hearing Fox's plan, as well as the recommendation of the military advisors, including Generals Scott and Totten, Lincoln called another cabinet meeting for March 15 and asked for each member of his cabinet to respond in writing about what should be done regarding Fort Sumter. All the cabinet members opposed in writing any reinforcement of Fort Sumter, except Postmaster General Blair, who offered to resign from the cabinet when the Fox plan was rejected.[44] Secretary of State Seward, who was generally considered the number two man to Lincoln, consistently opposed any reinforcement of Fort Sumter because he thought it would initiate a war with the South. His written note to the president contained these words:

> Suppose the expedition successful, we have then a garrison in Fort Sumter that can defy assault for six months. What is it to do then? Is it to make war by opening its batteries and attempting to demolish the defenses of the Carolinians? . . . I may be asked whether I would in no case, and at no time advise force—whether I propose to give up everything? I reply no. *I would not initiate war to regain a useless and unnecessary position on the soil of the seceding States.*[45]

Secretary of Treasury Chase said in his note to the president:

> *If the attempt will so inflame civil war* as to involve an immediate necessity for the enlistment of armies and the expedition of millions, I cannot advise it in the existing circumstances of the country and in the present condition of the national finances.[46]

Secretary of War Cameron advised against reinforcement with these words:

---

[43]Ibid., p. 166.

[44]Ibid., p. 167.

[45]Edgar Lee Masters, *Lincoln, The Man* (Columbia, S.C.: The Foundation for American Education, 1997), p. 392; emphasis added.

[46]Ibid.; emphasis added.

Whatever might have been done as late as a month ago, it is too sadly evident that it cannot now be done without the sacrifice of life and treasure not at all commensurate with the object to be attained; and as the abandonment of the fort in a few weeks, sooner or later, appears to be an inevitable necessity, it seems to me that the sooner it is done the better.[47]

Cameron also stated that:

The proposition presented by Mr. Fox, so sincerely entertained and ably advocated, would be entitled to my favorable consideration if, with all the light before me and in the face of so many distinguished military authorities on the other side, I did not believe that *the attempt to carry it into effect would initiate a bloody and protracted conflict.*[48]

Secretary of the Navy Wells opposed either sending *provisions* or reinforcing the fort with troops and stated:

By sending, or attempting to send provisions into Sumter, will not war be precipitated? It may be impossible to escape it under any course of policy that may be pursued, *but I am not prepared to advise a course that would provoke hostilities.* It does not appear to me that the dignity, strength, or character of the government will be promoted by an attempt to provision Sumter in the manner proposed, even should it succeed, while a failure would be attended with untold disaster.[49]

Attorney General Bates opposed the plan with these words:

The possession of the fort, as we now hold it, *does not enable us to collect the revenue* or enforce the laws of commercial navigation. It may indeed involve a point of honor or a point of pride, but I do not see any great national interest involved in the bare fact of holding the fort as we now hold it.[50]

---

[47]Ibid., pp. 392–93.
[48]Tilley, *Lincoln Takes Command*, p. 171; emphasis added.
[49]Masters, *Lincoln, The Man*, p. 393; emphasis added.
[50]Ibid.; emphasis added.

General Scott and General Totten both appeared before the cabinet meeting, and Scott submitted a written memorandum stating his military opinion. He not only opposed the Fox plan, but recommended that Forts Sumter and Pickens be evacuated immediately. He further stated that Captain Fox's plan of *simply making the attempt to approach the Fort with the ships "will inevitably involve a collision."*[51] Scott further pointed out that even if the plan was successful, they would not be able to hold the fort for any appreciable time. General Scott stated also that the evacuation of Forts Sumter and Pickens would strongly impress the eight remaining slave states that had not seceded and this might hold them in the Union.[52] President Lincoln received the advice both from the military officers and his cabinet and, with only one member of the cabinet supporting the plan, it was determined not to implement the Fox plan since the mere attempt to initiate the plan would undoubtedly cause a war.

Charles W. Ramsdell, in his excellent study of all the official records and diaries of the people involved, also points out:

> One plan which he [Lincoln] seems to have entertained for a short while, just after the adverse cabinet vote on relieving Sumter, contemplated the collection of customs duties on revenue vessels, supported by ships of war, just outside the Confederate ports; and there were hints in the press that Anderson's force was to be withdrawn to a ship off Charleston. If it were seriously considered, the plan was soon abandoned, possibly because of legal impediments or more probably because it did not fully meet the needs of the situation.[53]

Fox was a very persistent person, however, and, subsequent to this cabinet meeting, he asked Lincoln if he could go to Fort Sumter before a final decision was made in order to see for himself the conditions that were there. Lincoln had General Scott authorize a visit by Fox to Charleston to meet with Major Anderson,

---

[51]Tilley, *Lincoln Takes Command*, p. 172; emphasis added.
[52]Ibid.
[53]Ramsdell, "Lincoln and Fort Sumter," p. 268.

which Fox did on March 22. Also on that date, President Lincoln authorized two personal delegates, S.A. Hurlbut and Ward H. Lamon, to go to South Carolina. Hurlbut was to determine if there was any Unionist sympathy within South Carolina and particularly in Charleston. Lamon was a longtime trusted friend of the president, having been his law partner, and he was to visit both Governor Pickens and Major Anderson at Fort Sumter.[54]

Fox met directly with Anderson, who informed him that it would be impossible to reinforce the fort from the sea. Anderson stated that the only way to reinforce the fort successfully would be to have a massive army come from Morris Island. Anderson further warned Fox that any attempts to send reinforcements from the sea would cause the South to fire, thereby causing an unnecessary war. *It would be a provocative act merely to make the attempt.*[55] Anderson also informed Fox that there was *no need for food*, as he had an agreement with Governor Pickens and merchants in Charleston to furnish fresh groceries and meat on a daily basis. Anderson had already written his superior officers in Washington, "I do hope that no attempt will be made by our friends to throw supplies in; their doing so would do more harm than good."[56]

Hurlbut found that there was no significant amount of Unionist sympathy in Charleston, and therefore it could not be depended upon for any assistance. Lamon met with Governor Pickens and represented to him that he had come to arrange for the removal of Major Anderson and his entire garrison, and even described the type of ships that would come later to remove the troops. He informed Governor Pickens that he would be coming back soon and personally participating in the removal of the troops.[57] Lamon also learned from Governor Pickens that any attempt to send any ships to Fort Sumter, even if only bringing

---

[54]Potter, *Lincoln and His Party in the Secession Crisis*, pp. 340–41.

[55]Tilley, *Lincoln Takes Command*, pp. 176–78.

[56]Ibid., p. 147.

[57]Potter, *Lincoln and His Party in the Secession Crisis*, p. 340.

supplies, would cause the South to fire on the fort.[58] In fact, both Hurlbut and Lamon reported back to the president the key information he was seeking and that would be essential for his cabinet meeting on March 29—that is, *even sending supplies would cause the South to fire on the fort.*[59]

Meanwhile, Congress was still in session and the U.S. Senate became interested in the negotiations and sent word to President Lincoln that they wanted to be informed about the matters regarding Fort Sumter. President Lincoln sent General Scott who testified that he had recommended abandonment of Fort Sumter and felt that this was imperative. The Senate then passed a resolution requesting that President Lincoln furnish them copies of all correspondence with Major Anderson, but Lincoln refused, claiming executive privilege in a document dated March 26, 1861.[60]

It became obvious to the public, and especially to those in Washington, D.C., that Lincoln's refusal to offer any peace proposal or to meet with the Confederate commissioners was preventing any negotiations between the North and the South. Therefore, two U.S. Supreme Court justices, Samuel Nelson from the North and John Campbell from the South, approached Secretary of State Seward, and offered themselves as intermediators to meet with the commissioners and Seward in order to communicate peace offers, etc., and attempt to resolve the difficulties without a war. Seward began meeting with the justices soon after the cabinet meeting on March 15, and at that time, Justice Campbell received specific authority from Seward to write to President Jefferson Davis informing him that Fort Sumter would be evacuated within five days.[61] Once the commissioners had received such a strong statement from Seward, they dropped the demand for

---

[58]Ramsdell, "Lincoln and Fort Sumter," p. 274.

[59]Bruce Catton, *The Coming Fury* (Garden City, N.Y.: Doubleday, 1961), pp. 281–82.

[60]Tilley, *Lincoln Takes Command*, p. 191.

[61]Potter, *Lincoln and His Party in the Secession Crisis*, p. 345.

recognition of the South by Lincoln. Again, on March 21, Justice Campbell passed along a second note from Seward which stated Sumter would be evacuated, and Seward promised a further statement. Finally, on March 22, there was a third note authorized by Seward to be passed from Justice Campbell to the commissioners, and this note stated, "I [Secretary of State Seward] have still unabated confidence that Fort Sumter will be evacuated."[62] On March 30, the commissioners received word from Governor Pickens that Lamon's visit with him on March 25 was a commitment from the Lincoln administration that Sumter would be evacuated soon and that Lamon had represented himself to Governor Pickens to be the personal delegate of President Lincoln.[63]

An extremely important cabinet meeting occurred, however, on March 29, which produced a completely different result than the cabinet meeting which had occurred on March 15. One day before this meeting on the 29th, President Lincoln told Fox that his plan regarding Sumter would be put into effect.[64] At the cabinet meeting on March 29, all but two of the cabinet members voted to reinforce Fort Sumter. Secretary of State Seward continued to oppose reinforcement, as did cabinet member Caleb Smith, and both called for evacuation of the troops.[65] Immediately following this cabinet meeting, Lincoln issued an order to Fox to prepare the expedition to leave for Fort Sumter no later than April 6.[66] Furthermore, Lincoln issued secret executive orders for troops to be assembled and for the warships to be made ready.[67]

A major question arises as to what happened between March 15 and March 29 to change the cabinet's position and why Lincoln would indicate to Fox on the day before the cabinet meeting of March 29 that the plan was to be put into effect. David Potter

---

[62]Ibid., p. 347.

[63]Ibid.

[64]Tilley, *Lincoln Takes Command*, pp. 197–99.

[65]Potter, *Lincoln and His Party in the Secession Crisis*, p. 361.

[66]Ibid.

[67]Tilley, *Lincoln Takes Command*, p. 197.

renders his opinion that at the cabinet meeting on March 29, it was decided that General Scott's recommendation to evacuate Sumter was more a political decision to keep in the border states, rather than a military opinion.[68] There is little evidence of this and overwhelming evidence that other factors caused the change. There had been speculation for some time in the Northern press that the Morrill Tariff might create a problem for the North if the South adopted a low tariff position. A good example is the *New-Haven Daily Register*, which editorialized on February 11, 1861, that:

> There never was a more ill-timed, injudicious and destructive measure proposed, (so far as northern interests are concerned) than the Morrill tariff bill, now pending before Congress. It proposes to greatly increase the duties on all imported goods, and in many articles to carry up the increase to the prohibitory point . . . so that while Congress is raising the duties for the Northern ports, the Southern Convention is doing away with all import duties for the Southern ports. . . . More than three fourths of the seafront of the Atlantic States—extending from the Chesapeake inclusive, to the furtherest boundary of Texas, would be beyond the reach of our Congress tariff. Their ports would invite the free trade of the world! And what would the high tariff be worth to us then, with only a one-fourth fragment of our former seacoast left?[69]

Tax historian Charles Adams analyzes this Northern realization of what the comparative tariffs of the North and South would do to their industries:

> The war started, not because of the high Morrill Tariff, but just the opposite: it was the low southern tariff, which created a free trade zone. That tariff and its economic consequences for the North—disastrous consequences—were what aroused the anger of northern commercial interests and turned their apathy

[68]Potter, *Lincoln and His Party in the Secession Crisis*, p. 363.

[69]Howard Cecil Perkins, ed., *Northern Editorials on Secession* (Gloucester, Mass: Peter Smith, 1964), vol. 2, pp. 589–91.

toward the seceding states into militant anger. It united the money interests in the North, and they were willing to back the president with the capital needed to carry on the war. Here is the scenario:

1.   On March 11, 1861, the Confederate Constitution was adopted. It created what was essentially a free trade zone in the Confederacy, in contrast to the new high-tax, protective zone in the North.

2.   Within less than two weeks, northern newspapers grasped the significance of this and switched from a moderate, conciliatory policy to a militant demand for immediate action.[70]

The New York *Evening Post*, a Republican newspaper, published an editorial on March 12 as follows:

There are some difficulties attending the collection of the revenue in the seceding states which it will be well to look at attentively.

That either the revenue from duties must be collected in the ports of the rebel states, or the ports must be closed to importations from abroad, it is generally admitted. If neither of these things be done, our revenue laws are substantially repealed; the sources which supply our treasury will be dried up; we shall have no money to carry on the government; the nation will become bankrupt before the next crop of corn is ripe. . . . Allow railroad iron to be entered at Savannah with the low duty of ten percent, which is all that the Southern Confederacy think of laying on imported goods, and not an ounce more would be imported at New York; the railways would be supplied from the southern ports.

What, then, is left for our government? Shall we let the seceding states repeal the revenue laws for the whole Union in this manner? Or will the government choose to consider all foreign commerce destined for these ports where we have no custom-houses and no collectors, as contraband, and stop it, when offering to enter the collection districts from which our authorities have been expelled? Or will the president call a

---

[70]Charles Adams, *Those Dirty Rotten Taxes*, pp. 102–03.

special session of Congress to do what the last unwisely failed to do—to abolish all ports of entry in the seceding states?[71]

The *Philadelphia Press*, on March 18, 1861, demanded a war by calling for a blockade of all Southern ports. The paper pointed out that the vast border from the Atlantic Ocean to West Texas would have no protective tariff and European goods would underprice Northern goods in Southern markets, and that this would ruin Northern business.[72] Previously, on January 15, 1861, the same paper had been against any military action, arguing that the South should be allowed to go peacefully, but this was before the Morrill Tariff passed with its call for a high protective tariff and the Southern Confederacy passed its Constitutional prohibition against protective tariffs.[73] The *New York Times* also changed its position over the tariff issue, and on March 22 and 23, stated, "At once shut up every Southern port, destroy its commerce, and bring utter ruin on the Confederate states. . . . A state of war would almost be preferable to the passive action the government had been following."[74]

The most explicit article on this issue which now faced the Lincoln administration appeared in the *Boston Transcript* for March 18, 1861:

> It does not require extraordinary sagacity to perceive that trade is perhaps the controlling motive operating to prevent the return of the seceding states to the Union which they have abandoned. Alleged grievances in regard to slavery were originally the causes for separation of the cotton states; but the mask has been thrown off and it is apparent that the people of the principal seceding states are now for commercial independence. They *dream* that the centres of traffic can be changed from Northern to Southern ports. The merchants of New Orleans, Charleston and Savannah are possessed with the idea

[71]Perkins, ed., *Northern Editorials on Secession*, pp. 598–601.
[72]Adams, *Those Dirty Rotten Taxes*, p. 103.
[73]Ibid.
[74]Ibid.

that New York, Boston, and Philadelphia may be shorn, in the future, of their mercantile greatness, by a revenue system verging on free trade. If the Southern Confederation is allowed to carry out a policy by which only a nominal duty is laid upon imports, no doubt the business of the chief Northern cities will be seriously injured thereby.

The difference is so great between the tariff of the Union and that of the Confederate States that the entire Northwest must find it to their advantage to purchase their imported goods at New Orleans rather than New York. In addition to this, the manufacturing interests of the country will suffer from the increased importation resulting from low duties. . . . The [government] would be false to its obligations if this state of things were not provided against.[75]

Lincoln was also getting pressure from the Radical Republicans, especially governors, that he needed to adopt a strong policy and go to war, if necessary, over Fort Sumter. Typical of the reaction of the Radical Republicans was a letter dated March 27, 1861, from J.H. Jordon to Secretary of Treasury Chase, which undoubtedly was discussed with the cabinet members along with many other letters and newspaper editorials on this subject. This letter read as follows:

In the name of God! Why not hold the Fort? Will reinforcing & holding it cause the rebels to attack it, and thus bring on "civil war"? What of it? That is just what the government ought to wish to bring about, and ought to do all it can . . . to bring about. Let them attack the Fort, if they will—it will then be *them* that commence the war.[76]

It was also being widely reported in the press that the reason the Republicans were showing up poorly in elections in Ohio, Connecticut, and Rhode Island was that the administration was showing a weakness by abandoning Fort Sumter. Rutherford B.

---

[75]Ibid., pp. 104–05; emphasis in the original.

[76]Ramsdell, "Lincoln and Fort Sumter," p. 272; emphasis in the original.

Hayes had declared, "Yes, giving up Fort Sumter is vexing. It hurts our little election, too."[77]

Charles W. Ramsdell considered the evidence and argued that Lincoln was in a terrible bind by getting military advice that the reinforcement or bringing supplies would be a failure, but that politically he could not afford to evacuate the fort. Ramsdell states: "Could the Southerners be *induced* to attack Sumter, to assume the aggressive and thus put themselves in the wrong in the eyes of the North and of the world?"[78] He continues, that if the South could be induced to start the war, then:

> The two wings of his party would unite, some at least of the Democrats would come to his support, even the border-state people might be held, if they could be convinced that the war was being forced by the secessionists. Unless he could unite them in defense of the authority of the government, the peaceable and the "stiff-backed" Republicans would split apart, the party would collapse, his administration would be a failure, and he would go down in history as a weak man who had allowed the Union to crumble in his hands. As things now stood, the only way by which the Union could be restored, his party and his administration saved, was by an unequivocal assertion of the authority of the government; that is, through war. But he must not openly assume the aggressive; that must be done by the secessionists.[79]

Lincoln, with over 60 percent of the vote against him and his party being one of many clashing ideas, knew that his minority party could fall apart under the crisis. Shelby Foote has described this dilemma and Lincoln's strategy:

> Walking the midnight corridors of the White House after the day-long din of office seekers and divided counsels, Lincoln

---

[77]Potter, *Lincoln and His Party in the Secession Crisis*, p. 342; emphasis in the original.

[78]Ramsdell, "Lincoln and Fort Sumter," p. 272; emphasis in the original.

[79]Ibid., pp. 272–73.

knew that his first task was to unite all these discordant ele-
ments, and he knew, too, that the most effective way to do this
was to await an act of aggression by the South, exerting in the
interim just enough pressure to provoke such an action, without exerting enough to justify it.[80]

On April 1, there was a flurry of activity in the Lincoln
administration. As already mentioned, Lincoln issued new executive orders for Fort Pickens to be reinforced as election results
came in which were unfavorable to the Republicans, who lost an
important election in Ohio.[81] Secretary of State Seward on this
day also recommended in writing that Lincoln start a war with
either France or Spain instead of the South. Seward pointed out
that there had been recent Spanish and French aggressions in
Mexico and Santo Domingo, and he recommended that Lincoln
demand explanations from Spain and France, and if satisfactory
explanations were not received, to declare war against them.[82]
Seward had already received much criticism in January of 1861,
when he stated that, "If the Lord would only give the United
States an excuse for a war with England, France, or Spain, that
would be the best means of reestablishing internal peace."[83]
Seward recognized the tremendous value to the Lincoln administration of having a war, since this would unite the Republican
Party, cause great power to flow to the president, and end most
dissent and opposition. Lincoln had also learned this when he
tried to oppose President Polk in the Mexican War. However,
Lincoln preferred a war with the South rather than England,
Spain, or France. Lincoln answered Seward's note of April 1 with
a note of his own on the same day, turning down the advice on

[80]Shelby Foote, *The Civil War: A Narrative, Fort Sumter to Perryville* (New York: Vintage Books, 1986), p. 44.

[81]Potter, *Lincoln and His Party in the Secession Crisis*, p. 341.

[82]Ibid., pp. 368–69; for original documents, see *Collected Works of Abra-ham Lincoln*, Roy P. Basler, ed., (New Brunswick, N.J.: Rutgers University Press, 1953–55), pp. 316–18, 136–37, 153–55. See also, Howard K. Beale, *Diary of Gideon Welles: Secretary of Navy Under Lincoln and Johnson* (New York: Norton, 1960), vol. 1, p. 37.

[83]Potter, *Lincoln and His Party in the Secession Crisis*, pp. 369–70.

foreign policy. Seward, in his note, had also criticized Lincoln for having no domestic policy, and Lincoln responded to this charge in the same note by reminding Seward that in his first Inaugural Address, he set out his policy, which was to hold the forts and collect the taxes, and he said at the time this would be done by force or invasion, if necessary.[84]

Meanwhile, the Confederate commissioners were detecting much military activity and becoming very suspicious of what Lincoln was doing secretly. On April 1, Justice Campbell went to Secretary of State Seward and demanded confirmation that Fort Sumter was to be abandoned, but at this point, he heard a different story which he considered a change in position. Seward now informed him that the president might desire to supply Fort Sumter with food and provisions but not reinforce it with troops. However, Seward stated that Lincoln "will not undertake to do so without first giving notice to Governor Pickens."[85] Now the Lincoln administration was taking a different position and making a distinction between providing food or supplies and reinforcing with troops by having the public believe that Major Anderson and his troops were "starving." However, Anderson continued to get daily supplies from Charleston until the South realized for certain that the North was sending troops and ships to precipitate an attack on Fort Sumter, and his food supplies were not cut off until April 7. Seward however, continued to guarantee to Justice Campbell that the cabinet and the president had decided to evacuate Fort Sumter eventually.[86] Seward informed Justice Campbell that the delay by the administration regarding evacuation was being forced because certain Republicans had asked the president to wait for an outcome of the elections in Connecticut and Rhode Island, and the administration had made a commitment to wait on those results.[87] Finally, on April 8, Justice Campbell pushed Seward for a response, as there

---

[84]Van Doren, ed., *The Literary Works of Abraham Lincoln*, pp. 183–84.
[85]Potter, *Lincoln and His Party in the Secession Crisis*, p. 347.
[86]Ibid., p. 348.
[87]Ibid.

was much rumor of military activity going on, and Seward sent a note to Campbell which stated, "Faith as to Sumter fully kept; wait and see."[88] On April 2, Confederate Secretary of State L.P. Walker, upon learning from the commissioners that there was much military activity and a rumor that the Lincoln administration might try to reinforce Fort Sumter, told General Beauregard in Charleston that he should consider discontinuing food supplies to Major Anderson.[89]

On April 3, Lincoln and Seward decided to send a delegate, Allen B. McGruder, to the Virginia Secession Convention to try to get a commitment from Virginia that it would not secede. On February 13, the state of Virginia had initiated a convention to consider the question of its secession and what to do about the seven states which had already seceded. There was strong sentiment against secession in Virginia, but it was obvious there was a very dangerous situation existing, especially regarding Forts Pickens and Sumter, with armed troops having guns trained on each other. The Buchanan administration was a lame duck administration, and it was unknown at that time how President Lincoln would deal with the crisis. Virginia was the key Southern state. There were seven other border states that also had not seceded, and they looked to Virginia for leadership.

McGruder was sent on April 4 to invite representatives of the convention to come to Washington and discuss these matters directly with President Lincoln. The convention chose three commissioners, but they were told that this must be a very secret mission, and since these individuals were so well-known in Washington, it was decided to send Colonel John B. Baldwin, who was well-known in Virginia but not in Washington. He was also a person known to be opposed to secession.[90] Colonel Baldwin's interview with Lincoln is related by Rev. R.L. Dabney,

---

[88] Ibid.

[89] Tilley, *Lincoln Takes Command*, p. 202.

[90] Robert L. Dabney, "Memoir of a Narrative Received of Colonel John B. Baldwin of Staunton, Touching the Origin of the War," *Discussions* (Harrisonburg, Va.: Sprinkle Publications, 1994), pp. 87–110.

based on a personal interview with Baldwin in 1865, but Baldwin also testified under oath before the Joint Commission of Reconstruction in the same year with the same testimony.[91] Colonel Baldwin reported that he met Secretary of State Seward on April 4, and was taken to the White House and introduced to President Lincoln. Lincoln was meeting in a room with numerous individuals, but after being told by Seward that Colonel Baldwin was present, he excused himself and went upstairs with Baldwin, locked the door, and had a private conversation.

Baldwin reported to Lincoln that Virginia wanted to stay in the Union and that this would help keep the other border states from joining the seven states which had seceded. The Virginia Convention was not worried about the issue of slavery, but it was worried about Lincoln using force to bring back the seceding states. Therefore, it wanted a written proclamation of not more than five lines to state simply that the Lincoln administration would uphold the Constitution and federal laws. The convention wanted a firm commitment that Lincoln would not use force to bring the states back. Baldwin reported further, that if Lincoln would sign such a proclamation, Virginia would not secede and would use its best efforts to get all the seceded states back into the Union. Then, Baldwin reported, Lincoln stood up and seemed very frustrated and stalked around the room and said, "I ought to have known this sooner! You are too late, sir, *too late!* Why did you not come here four days ago, and tell me all this?"[92] Baldwin protested that he came as soon as he was invited to do so and he got here as soon as possible. Lincoln again replied: "Yes, but you are too late, I tell you, *too late!*"[93]

Baldwin then related that he came to the conclusion that a policy of compulsion had already been decided upon and it was too late to stop it. Baldwin stated that Lincoln seemed to be impressed with the sincerity with which he reported that Virginia

---

[91]Potter, *Lincoln and His Party in the Secession Crisis*, pp. 354–58 and see footnote 47, p. 357.

[92]Dabney, *Discussions*, p. 92; emphasis in the original.

[93]Ibid.; emphasis in the original.

wanted to stay in the Union and that the Virginians would use their best efforts to try to bring the seceded states back; however, Lincoln asked him, "But what am I to do in the meantime with those men at Montgomery? Am I to let them go on?"[94] Baldwin replied, "Yes sir, until they can be peaceably brought back."[95] Lincoln then replied, "And open Charleston, etc., as ports of entry, with their ten-percent tariff. *What, then, would become of my tariff?*"[96]

Baldwin concluded sadly that there could be no agreement on the part of Lincoln about a commitment not to use force, so he returned to Virginia and reported his findings to the three commissioners and to the convention. The three Virginia commissioners then decided to go to Washington and meet with Lincoln. They spoke directly with Lincoln in the White House and again urged forbearance and evacuation of the forts. Lincoln objected that all goods would then be imported through Charleston and his source of revenue would be dried up. His statement was, "If I do that, what would become of my revenue? I might as well shut up housekeeping at once!"[97]

Baldwin also told Reverend Dabney that, after the war, he had talked with a personal friend and apologist of Secretary of State Seward, and Baldwin inquired as to why Seward had misled Justice Campbell of the U.S. Supreme Court about Lincoln's intentions concerning Fort Sumter, as well as misleading the Confederate commissioners. The friend of Seward stated that Lincoln was swayed from taking Seward's and General Scott's advice about Fort Sumter by "Thad. Stevens and the radical governors."[98] Colonel Baldwin continued with the statement from Seward's friend, who stated that there was "great wrath" shown by the radical governors and they spoke to Lincoln as follows:

---

[94]Ibid., p. 94.

[95]Ibid.

[96]Ibid.; emphasis in the original.

[97]Ibid., p. 97.

[98]Ibid., p. 98.

Seward cries perpetually that we must not do this, and that, for fear war should result. Seward is shortsighted. War is precisely the thing we should desire. Our party interests have everything to lose by a peaceable settlement of this trouble, and everything to gain by collision. For a generation we have been "the outs"; now at last we are "the ins." While in opposition, it was very well to prate of the Constitution, and of rights; but now we are the government, and mean to continue so; and our interest is to have a strong and centralized government. It is high time now that the government were revolutionized and consolidated, and these irksome "States' rights" wiped out. We need a strong government to dispense much wealth and power to its adherents; we want permanently high tariffs, to make the South tributary to the North; and now these Southern fellows are giving us precisely the opportunity we want to do all this, and shall Seward sing his silly song of the necessity of avoiding war? War is the very thing we should hail! The Southern men are rash, and now profoundly irritated. Our plan should be, by some artifice, to provoke them to seem to strike the first blow. Then we shall have a pretext with which to unite the now divided North, and make them fly to arms. The Southerners are a braggart, but a cowardly and effeminate set of bullies; we shall easily whip them in three months. But this short war will be, if we are wise, our sufficient occasion. We will use it to destroy slavery, and thus permanently cripple the South. And that is the stronghold of all these ideas of "limited government" and "rights of the people." Crush the South, by abolishing slavery, and we shall have all we want—a consolidated government, an indefinite party ascendancy, and ability to lay on such tariffs and taxes as we please, and aggrandize ourselves and our section![99]

On April 4, Martin J. Crawford, who was one of the Confederate commissioners, telegraphed Governor Pickens expressing his opinion that the president intended to shift the responsibility to Major Anderson by simply taking no action and leaving Anderson to make his own decisions. Governor Pickens had also, on the same day, received word from the Confederate government that the food supplies from Charleston to Major Anderson should be

---

[99]Ibid., pp. 98–99.

cut off. Therefore, Governor Pickens sent a messenger to Major Anderson at Fort Sumter telling him that the privilege of getting food supplies from Charleston would end soon, and he also relayed the information he had received from Mr. Crawford, in order to tell Anderson what was being said in Washington. The rumor reported to Major Anderson was that: "Mr. Lincoln would not order Major Anderson to withdraw from Fort Sumter, and would leave him to act for himself."[100] The messenger reported back to Governor Pickens that Anderson became extremely upset with the report. Anderson's written reply of April 5 is part of the official records and was sent to his superiors in Washington reporting the rumor and asking if it was true that he was to be abandoned without any orders. It appears clear from this that Major Anderson did not know that any reinforcements were being sent. In his report he states that his food supplies were soon to be cut off from Charleston.[101] As we know now, Lincoln had already issued the orders to reinforce Fort Sumter and was using the pretext that he was "sending bread to the starving garrison," when in fact, it was not until April 7 that the South cut off Anderson's food supply, and this was entirely the result of provocative acts of the president.[102] Also, Anderson had previously let it be known that even if his supplies were cut off from Charleston, he would still have enough food to last until April 26.

On April 7, the *New York Herald* published the substance of a message from Confederate President Jefferson Davis:

> Dispatches received here to-day from Montgomery render it perfectly certain that no attack will be made by the Confederate troops on either Fort Sumter or Fort Pickens. President Davis is determined that this administration shall not place him in a false position, by making it appear to the world that the South is the aggressor. This has been and still is the policy of Mr. Lincoln. It will not be successful. Unless Mr. Lincoln's

---

[100]Tilley, *Lincoln Takes Command*, p. 211.

[101]Ibid., p. 212.

[102]Stampp, *And the War Came: The North and the Secession Crisis, 1860–1861*, p. 282.

administration makes the first demonstration and attack, President Davis says there will be no collision or bloodshed. *With the Lincoln administration, therefore, rests the responsibility of precipitating a collision*, and the fearful evils of protracted civil war.[103]

Furthermore, on April 7, Major Anderson received a letter composed by President Lincoln but signed by Secretary of War Cameron that was dated April 4, which informed Anderson that Lincoln was actually sending troops and ships to reinforce Fort Sumter. Anderson had warned Lincoln earlier that any successful reinforcement would have to be done by sending in thousands of troops from Fort Moultrie and that any reinforcement attempt from the sea would not be successful and would only cause the South to fire on the fort, and this would start a war.

On April 8, Anderson composed a letter to be sent back to President Lincoln; however, the South had not only cut off his food supply at this point but also confiscated all the mail delivery, including this letter which read, in part, as follows:

> I had the honor to receive by yesterday's mail the letter of the honorable Secretary of War, dated April 4, and confess that what he there states surprises me very greatly, following as it does in contradicting so positively the assurance Mr. Crawford telegraphed he was authorized to make. I trust that this matter will be at once put in a correct light, as a movement made now, when the South has been erroneously informed that none such will be attempted, would produce most disastrous results throughout our country.
>
> We have not oil enough to keep a light in the lantern for one night. The boats will have, therefore, to rely at night entirely upon other marks. I ought to have been informed that this expedition was to come. Colonel Lamon's remark convinced me that the idea, merely hinted at to me by Captain Fox, would not be carried out. We shall strive to do our duty, though I frankly say that *my heart is not in the war which I see is to be thus commenced.* That God will still avert it, and cause us to resort

---

[103]Tilley, *Lincoln Takes Command*, p. 219; emphasis in the original.

to pacific measures to maintain our rights, is my ardent prayer.[104]

By intercepting this letter, the South now knew that Lincoln was not just sending food supplies but was sending massive forces for the reinforcement of Fort Sumter in complete violation of all assurances previously made. They knew that great deception had been practiced by Lincoln in his representations to various agents of the Confederacy. President Davis now understood, not only from this letter, but also other sources, that Lincoln was sending a threatening army of reinforcements in the form of eight ships, with twenty-six cannons and fourteen hundred men, which would arrive in Charleston within a few days.[105] Also on April 8, a special messenger from President Lincoln, by the name of Robert L. Chew, a mere clerk in the State Department rather than an official, arrived in Charleston and went with Captain Theo Talbot to meet with Governor Pickens. Mr. Chew delivered a written message composed by Lincoln which stated:

> I am directed by the President of the United States to notify you to expect an attempt will be made to supply Fort Sumter with provisions only; and that, if such an attempt be not resisted, no effort to throw in men, arms, or ammunition will be made without further notice, or in case of an attack upon the fort.[106]

On April 10, the New York *Tribune* published an editorial which stated, "We are enabled to state, *with positive certainty*, that the principal object of the military and naval expedition which has sailed from this harbor, within the past four days, is *the relief of Fort Sumter*."[107] As soon as the editorial appeared, the three Confederate commissioners in Washington telegraphed General Beauregard in Charleston that the "The *Tribune* of to-day declares the

---

[104]Ibid., pp. 223–24; emphasis added.

[105]Jefferson Davis, *Rise and Fall of the Confederate Government* (Nashville, Tenn: William Mayes Coats, 1996), vol. 1, p. 284.

[106]Ramsdell, "Lincoln and Fort Sumter," p. 280.

[107]Tilley, *Lincoln Takes Command*, p. 230; emphasis in the original.

main object of the expedition to be the relief of Sumter, and that a force will be landed which will overcome all opposition."[108]

Meanwhile, in Montgomery, Secretary of War Leroy Walker had received word from General Beauregard in Charleston that Governor Pickens had received an official notice through Robert Chew from President Lincoln, that the reinforcements were coming, and Walker sent a telegram back to Beauregard stating:

> If you have no doubt of the authorized character of the agent who communicated to you the intention of the Washington Government to supply Fort Sumter by force you will at once demand its evacuation, and if this is refused proceed, in such manner as you may determine, to reduce it.[109]

The next day General Beauregard sent two representatives to deliver a message to Major Anderson at Fort Sumter and asked if he would immediately evacuate the fort, and if he agreed to do so, they would allow him to do so with honor and without harm. Anderson sent back a reply in writing that he refused to leave, but he stated orally to the messengers "I will await the first shot, and if you do not batter us to pieces, we will be starved out in a few days."[110] General Beauregard and the South's military leaders all knew that Lincoln's ships and armed forces would arrive no later than April 12, and probably sooner. Therefore, they reasoned that they were left with no alternative but to tell Major Anderson they could not wait any longer, and if he did not evacuate now, they would begin firing on April 12.

Bruce Catton, a prominent Civil War historian, explains how Lincoln maneuvered Davis into firing the first shot:

> Lincoln had been plainly warned by Lamon and by Hurlbut that a ship taking provisions to Fort Sumter would be fired on. Now he was sending the ship, with advance notice to the men who had the guns. He was sending war ships and soldiers as well, but

---

[108]Ibid.
[109]Ibid., p. 231.
[110]Ibid., p. 233.

they would remain in the background; if there was going to be a war it would begin over a boat load of salt pork and crackers—over that, and the infinite overtones which by now were involved. Not for nothing did Captain Fox remark afterward that it seemed very important to Lincoln that South Carolina "should stand before the civilized world as having fired upon bread."[111]

One biographer of Jefferson Davis, Robert McElroy, described the thinking of Davis and his cabinet in sending the order to fire on Sumter: "The order [by Lincoln] for the sending of the fleet was a declaration of war."[112] Shelby Foote describes the dilemma as follows:

Lincoln had maneuvered them into the position of having either to back down on their threats or else to fire the first shot of the war. What was worse, in the eyes of the world, that first shot would be fired for the immediate purpose of keeping food from hungry men.

Davis assembled his cabinet and laid the message before them. Their reactions were varied. Robert Toombs, the fire-eater, was disturbed and said so: "The firing on that fort will inaugurate a civil war greater than any the world has yet seen, and I do not feel competent to advise you." He paced the room, head lowered, hands clasped beneath his coattails. "Mr. President, at this time it is suicide, murder, and you will lose us every friend at the North. You will wantonly strike a hornets' nest which extends from mountains to ocean. Legions now quiet will swarm out and sting us to death. It is unnecessary. It puts us in the wrong. It is fatal."

Davis reasoned otherwise, and made his decision accordingly. It was not he who had forced the issue, but Lincoln, and this the world would see and know, along with the deception which had been practiced.[113]

---

[111]Catton, *The Coming Fury*, p. 297.
[112]Tilley, *Lincoln Takes Command*, p. 263.
[113]Foote, *The Civil War*, pp. 47–48.

The logic of Davis was reasonable in light of all he knew about the negotiations over Pickens and Sumter. He knew Lincoln had decided not to abandon the forts and was prepared to send in reinforcements. It would not have been reasonable to wait until the forts had been resupplied and reinforced with men and ammunition before firing on them. Davis could not have a federal fort left in Charleston harbor after secession any more than the American colonists could have allowed the British to continue having a fort in the New York or Boston harbors after secession from England. It was clear that Lincoln had deceived the South in his various promises, especially through Seward, to evacuate the forts. Now he was clearly provoking a war by resupplying Fort Sumter and showing thereby that it would not be evacuated. However, the public did not have the benefit of all the information concerning negotiations over the forts and did not understand all the correspondence that had gone back and forth to indicate clearly that the sending of the ships for reinforcement, or sending them bread, was to be considered an act of war by the South. The public simply saw what appeared to be an innocent act of "sending bread to the starving garrison," and the South opened fire. If the South had won the war, Davis's viewpoint would have been in the history books along with the reasons the North would not allow the South to secede. But nothing is more certain in history than the fact that the winners write it.

When the South commenced firing, in the early morning hours of April 12, the first Lincoln ship, *The Harriet Lane*, had arrived near the Charleston harbor. The South continued to fire upon the fort for thirty-six hours and during this time the remainder of the ships arrived. However, the ships never returned any fire, indicating their mission had been accomplished simply by drawing the first shot from the South.

Many newspapers in the North reacted to the firing on Fort Sumter and Lincoln's deception in provoking the South to fire the first shot. Representative of these reports in the North is an editorial in the *Buffalo Daily Courier*, dated April 16, 1861.

The news of the fall of Fort Sumter has been received at the North more with astonishment than any other feeling. Every mind is full of questions. Has the administration been in earnest in this first strangely disastrous battle? If the fort was to be rein-forced, why was not the attempt made? . . . The affair at Fort Sumter, it seems to us, has been planned as a means by which the war feeling at the North should be intensified, and the adminis-tration thus receive popular support for its policy. . . . If the arma-ment which lay outside the harbor, while the fort was being bat-tered to pieces, had been designed for the relief of Major Anderson, it certainly would have made a show of fulfilling its mission. But it seems plain to us that no such design was had. The administration, virtually, to use a homely illustration, stood at Sumter like a boy with a chip on his shoulder, daring his antago-nist to knock it off. The Carolinians have knocked off the chip. War is inaugurated, and the design of the administration is accomplished.[114]

The New York *Evening Day-Book*, in its editorial dated April 17, stated as follows:

We have no doubt, and all the circumstances prove, that it was a cunningly devised scheme, contrived with all due attention to scenic display and intended to arouse, and, if possible, exas-perate the northern people against the South. Lincoln and Seward know very well that the right to send a vessel with pro-visions to Major Anderson *involved just the same issue as a rein-forcement*. Hence it was made in a way that enabled them to get up a story about "humanity," "relieving a starving garri-son." It would be impossible for Seward to do anything openly and above board.

We venture to say a more gigantic conspiracy against the principles of human liberty and freedom has never been con-cocted. Who but a fiend could have thought of sacrificing the gallant Major Anderson and his little band in order to carry out a political game? Yet there he was compelled to stand for thirty-six hours amid a torrent of fire and shell, while the fleet sent to assist him, coolly looked at his flag of distress and moved not to his assistance! Why did they not? Perhaps the archives at Washington will yet tell the tale of this strange pro-ceeding.

---

[114]Perkins, *Northern Editorials on Secession*, p. 716.

Pause then, and consider before you endorse these mad men who are now, under pretense of preserving the Union, doing the very thing that must forever divide it.[115]

The *Providence Daily Post*, on April 13, 1861 editorialized as follows:

We are to have civil war, if at all, because Abraham Lincoln loves a [the Republican] party better than he loves his country. . . . [He] clings to his party creed, and allows the nation to drift into the whirlpool of destruction. While commerce is languishing, and all our industrial interests are threatened with ruin, he calls upon the people of the North—Democrats, Conservatives, and Republicans—to march to the South, and vindicate—what? The national honor? By no means; but the Chicago platform! . . . The cotton States, despairing of justice under such circumstances, have withdrawn from the Union, asking only to be let alone.

We are told, however, just now, that war results, if at all, from an act of humanity on the part of our government—that the garrison at Fort Sumter needs food, and the effort is to supply them. That is all. Is it all? Look at the facts. For three weeks the administration newspapers have been assuring us that Fort Sumter would be abandoned. They said it could not be provisioned or reinforced without a great sacrifice of life, and without greatly exasperating the whole South; that to abandon it would certainly disappoint and embarrass the secessionist, and kill the spirit of secession in all the border slave States. They had got the public mind all ready for the event, when—*presto!*—the tables are turned, and Fort Sumter is to be provisioned! Secession is *not* to be killed! Why?

We think the reader will perceive why. Mr. Lincoln saw an opportunity to inaugurate civil war without appearing in the character of an aggressor. There are men in Fort Sumter, he said, who are nearly out of provisions. They ought to be fed. We will attempt to feed them. Certainly nobody can blame us for that. We ought to feed our gallant soldiers by all means. *We will* attempt to feed them. The secessionists, who are both mad and

---

[115]Ibid., pp. 718–19; emphasis in the original.

foolish, will resist us. Then will commence civil war. Then I will appeal to the North to aid me in putting down rebellion, and the North must respond. How can it do otherwise?[116]

Finally, another representative editorial from the Northern press comes from New Jersey and the Jersey City *American Standard*. This was published on the day of the firing on Fort Sumter, April 12, 1861:

There is a madness and a ruthlessness in the course which is attributed to the government which is astounding. It would seem as if it were bent upon the destruction instead of the preservation of the Union, and as if all wisdom and patriotism had departed from it, or had been forced to succumb to the demands of its infuriated partisan leaders. . . . [T]he government seeks to mask this, its real purpose, by pretending that humanity requires them to succor the gallant Major Anderson and his troops, and that an unarmed vessel is to be sent to him with stores and that if it is not permitted peaceably to fulfill its errand it shall be done by force. The measure is a disingenuous feint. . . . This unarmed vessel, it is well understood, is a mere decoy to draw the first fire from the people of the South, which act by the pre-determination of the government is to be the pretext for letting loose the horrors of war. It dare not itself fire the first shot or draw the first blood, and is now seeking by a mean artifice to transfer the odium of doing so to the Southern Confederacy. . . . The assumption of a regard for humanity and the actions which the government base upon it are a sham the most transparent, a mockery the most unsubstantial, an hypocrisy which is only more infamous than the low cunning with which it is commingled.

No intelligent man will be deceived by the plea, and if blood be shed it will be laid where it justly ought to be laid, at the door of an Administration which had not the courage to surrender an abstraction in order to preserve the peace and unity of the country, but was brave enough to dare to close its ear against all the persuasive ties of common brotherhood, a common country, a common ancestry, a common religion and a

---

[116]Ibid., pp. 711–13; emphasis in the original.

common language, and by plunging the nation into civil war to demolish the noble fabric which our fathers founded.

If this result follows—and follow civil war it must—the memory of ABRAHAM LINCOLN and his infatuated advisors will only be preserved with that of other destroyers to be scorned and execrated. . . . And if the historian who preserves the record of his fatal administration needs any motto descriptive of the president who destroyed the institutions which he swore to protect, it will probably be some such an one as this:

Here is the record of one who feared more to have it said that he deserted his party than that he ruined his country, who had a greater solicitude for his consistency as a partisan than for his wisdom as a Statesman or his courage and virtue as a patriot, and who destroyed by his weakness the fairest experiment of man in self government that the world ever witnessed.[117]

There were no casualties on either side as a result of the bombardment of Fort Sumter, and after the firing ended, the South sent a doctor to see if Anderson needed his services. Major Anderson replied that there were no injuries or casualties and he needed no assistance, but he did request, and was then allowed, to have a ceremony to lower the flag and to leave with honor. However, during this ceremony, one of his cannons exploded and a Northern soldier was killed, which was the only casualty involved in the Fort Sumter incident.

Shelby Foote records the respect which both sides demonstrated toward each other, and especially the Southerners who admired the bravery of Major Anderson and his troops for enduring the assault. Foote states, "As the weary artillerymen passed silently out of the harbor, Confederate soldiers lining the beaches removed their caps in salute. There was no cheering."[118] The matter could have ended here with only one accidental death. The South would have seceded and preserved the ideas of a limited

---

[117]Ibid., pp. 706–08; emphasis in the original.

[118]Foote, *The Civil War: A Narrative, Fort Sumter to Perryville*, p. 50.

central government and states' rights advocated by the Founding Fathers. Slavery would have died a natural death soon, without a war, as it did everywhere else in Western civilization. Instead, President Lincoln, without consulting Congress, called for seventy-five thousand militia and unconstitutionally invaded the South as a "retaliation" for the firing on Fort Sumter. Also, on April 15, Lincoln called for Congress to meet, but not until July 4, 1861. Without any threat to the government in Washington or to the North, Lincoln began the war through illegal and unconstitutional means, claiming he was acting under the "war powers" of the president set out in the Constitution.

Since Congress never declared war, the question has arisen as to when the Civil War started. The U.S. Supreme Court was called on to decide this question in several cases which arose both during and immediately after the war. The popular opinion has been that the war officially started when the South fired on Fort Sumter; however, the Supreme Court stated that the war had two starting dates subsequent to the Fort Sumter incident, both initiated by President Lincoln in calling for a blockade of Southern ports. The first Presidential Proclamation was issued on April 19, 1861, applying to South Carolina, Georgia, Alabama, Florida, Mississippi, Louisiana, and Texas; the second, issued on April 27, 1861, applied to Virginia and North Carolina.[119]

After the Fort Sumter incident, Justice Campbell of the U.S. Supreme Court realized that he had been badly misled by Secretary of State Seward during their negotiations, and he wrote to Seward criticizing him for this deception:

> I think no candid man who will read what I have written and consider for a moment what is going on at Sumter but will agree that the equivocating conduct of the Administration, as measured and interpreted in connection with these promises, is the proximate cause of the great calamity.[120]

---

[119]James G. Randall, *Constitutional Problems Under Lincoln* (Chicago: University of Chicago Press, 1951), p. 50.

[120]Tilley, *Lincoln Takes Command*, p. 288.

Secretary of State Seward never responded to this letter; however, his biographer, Thornton K. Lothrop, revealed Seward's opinion about Sumter: "The Sumter expedition failed of its ostensible object, but it brought about the Southern attack on that fort. The first gun fired there effectively cleared the air . . . and placed Lincoln at the head of the united people."[121]

Charles Ramsdell, a prominent historian, argues convincingly that Lincoln's whole purpose in using the Fox plan was to prompt the South into firing the first shot:

> Although there were no casualties during the bombardment, the mere news that the attack on the fort had begun swept the entire North into a roaring flame of anger. The "rebels" had fired the first shot; they had chosen to begin war. If there had been any doubt earlier whether the mass of the Northern people would support the administration in suppressing the secessionists, there was none now. Lincoln's strategy had been completely successful. He seized at once the psychological moment for calling out the militia and committing the North to support of the war. This action cost him four of the border slave states, but he had probably already discounted that loss.[122]

Lincoln never ceased to blame the South for causing the war, and even in his State of the Union Address on December 6, 1864, Lincoln stated, "In stating a simple condition of peace, I mean simply to say that the war will cease on the part of the Government whenever it shall have ceased on the part of *those who began it*."[123]

After the war, Confederate President Jefferson Davis explained his reasons for giving the order to fire on Fort Sumter:

> The attempt to represent us as the *aggressors* in the conflict which ensued is as unfounded as the complaint made by the wolf against the lamb in the familiar fable. He who makes the assault is not necessarily he that strikes the first blow or fires the

---

[121]Ibid., p. 265.

[122]Ramsdell, "Lincoln and Fort Sumter," pp. 284–85.

[123]Tilley, *Lincoln Takes Command*, p. 227; emphasis added.

first gun. To have awaited further strengthening of their position by land and naval forces, with hostile purpose now declared, for the sake of having them "fire the first gun," would have been as unwise as it would be to hesitate to strike down the arm of the assailant, who levels a deadly weapon at one's breast, until he has actually fired. The disingenuous rant of demagogues about "firing on the flag" might serve to rouse the passions of insensate mobs in times of general excitement, but will be impotent in impartial history to relieve the Federal Government from the responsibility of the assault made by sending a hostile fleet against the harbor of Charleston, to cooperate with the menacing garrison of Fort Sumter. After the assault was made by the hostile descent of the fleet, the reduction of Fort Sumter was a measure of defense rendered absolutely and immediately necessary.

Such clearly was the idea of the commander of the *Pawnee*, when he declined, as Captain Fox informs us, without orders from a superior, to make any effort to enter the harbor, "there to inaugurate civil war." The straightforward simplicity of the sailor had not been perverted by the shams of political sophistry.

But, suppose the Confederate authorities had been disposed to yield, and to consent to the introduction of supplies for the maintenance of the garrison, what assurance would they have had that nothing further would be attempted? What reliance could be placed in any assurances of the Government of the United States after the experience of the attempted *ruse* of the *Star of the West* and the deceptions practiced upon the Confederate Commissioners in Washington? He says we were "expressly notified" that nothing more "would *on that occasion* be attempted"—the words in italics themselves constituting a very significant though unobtrusive and innocent-looking limitation. But we have been just as expressly notified, long before, that the garrison would be withdrawn. It would be as easy to violate the one pledge as it had been to break the other.

Moreover, the so-called notification was a mere memorandum, without date, signature, or authentication of any kind, sent to Governor Pickens, not by an accredited agent, but by a subordinate employee of the State Department. Like the oral and written pledges of Mr. Seward, given through Judge Campbell, it seemed to be carefully and purposely divested of every attribute that could make it binding and valid, in case its authors should see fit to repudiate it.[124]

President Davis went on to say:

> The bloodless bombardment and surrender of Fort Sumter occurred on April 13, 1861. The garrison was generously permitted to retire with the honors of war. The evacuation of that fort, commanding the entrance to the harbor of Charleston, which, if in hostile hands, was destructive of its commerce, had been claimed as the right of South Carolina. The voluntary withdrawal of the garrison by the United States Government had been considered, and those best qualified to judge believed it had been promised. Yet, when instead of the fulfillment of just expectations, instead of the withdrawal of the garrison, a hostile expedition was organized and sent forward, the urgency of the case required its reduction before it should be reinforced. Had there been delay, the more serious conflict between larger forces, land and naval, would scarcely have been bloodless, as the bombardment fortunately was. The event, however, was seized upon to inflame the mind of the Northern people, and the disguise which had been worn in the communications with the Confederate Commissioners was now thrown off, and it was cunningly attempted to show that the South, which had been pleading for peace and still stood on the defensive, had by this bombardment inaugurated a war against the United States.[125]

Following the maneuver of getting the South to fire the first shot and "start the war," Lincoln then set out to become America's first dictator. One of his strongest supporters, historian Arthur M. Schlesinger, Jr., describes Lincoln's initial conduct of the war as follows:

---

[124]Davis, *The Rise and Fall of the Confederate Government*, vol. 1, pp. 292–95; emphasis in the original.

[125]Ibid., pp. 297. Also, see explanation of Confederate Vice President Alexander H. Stephens, *A Constitutional View of the War Between the States* (Harrisonburg, Va.: Sprinkle Publications, 1994), vol. 2, pp. 34–36, 349. For another compact and reasonable interpretation of Lincoln's first shot maneuver, see Stampp, *And the War Came*, pp. 263–86.

Lincoln chose nevertheless to begin by assuming power to act independently of Congress. Fort Sumter was attacked on April 12, 1861. On April 15, Lincoln summoned Congress to meet in special session—but not until July 4. He thereby gained ten weeks to bypass Congress, ruled by decree, and set the nation irrevocably on the path to war.

On April 15, he called out state militia to the number of seventy-five thousand. Here he was acting on the basis of a statute. From then on he acted on his own. On April 19, he imposed a blockade on rebel ports, thereby assuming authority to take actions hitherto considered as requiring a declaration of war. On May 3, he called for volunteers and enlarged the army and navy, thereby usurping the power confided to Congress to raise armies and maintain navies. On April 20, he ordered the Secretary of Treasury to spend public money for defense without congressional appropriation, thereby violating Article I, section 9, of the Constitution. On April 27, he authorized the commanding general of the army to suspend the writ of *habeas corpus*—this despite the fact that the power of suspension, while not assigned explicitly to Congress, lay in that article of the Constitution devoted to the powers of Congress and was regarded by commentators before Lincoln as a congressional prerogative. Later he claimed the *habeas corpus* clause as a precedent for wider suspension of constitutional rights in time of rebellion or invasion—an undoubted stretching of original intent.[126]

The question that history must eventually determine is whether Lincoln maneuvered the South into firing the first shot in order that the public would believe, and history would record, that the South started the war which Lincoln actually started and wanted? While Lincoln was a very manipulative and secretive person, there is hard evidence which clearly indicts him of this offense. Not only do the official records, revealed particularly by

---

[126]Arthur M. Schlesinger, Jr., "War and the Constitution: Abraham Lincoln and Franklin D. Roosevelt," in *Lincoln The War President: The Gettysburg Lectures,* Gabor S. Boritt, ed. (New York: Oxford University Press, 1992), pp. 155–56; Also for other details of Lincoln's unconstitutional conduct see James G. Randall, *Constitutional Problems Under Lincoln.*

the study of John Shipley Tilley, indicate this, but Lincoln himself leaves the evidence.[127] First, there is his letter to Gustavus Fox dated May 1, 1865, in which he consoled Fox and told him he should not be worried about the fact that his attempt to bring supplies to Fort Sumter was unsuccessful. Lincoln assured him that he still had confidence in him and praised him for the effort. Lincoln states in his letter,

> You and I both anticipated that the cause of the country would be advanced by making the attempt to provision Fort Sumter, even if it should fail; and it is no small consolation now to feel that our anticipation is justified by the result.[128]

Lincoln also demonstrated his appreciation to Fox by elevating him to a high position of assistant secretary of the Navy in 1865.[129] Second, Lincoln's two trusted confidential secretaries, John G. Nicolay and John Hay, recorded their accounts of Lincoln's efforts to get the South to fire the first shot. One of their references states, "Abstractly it was enough that the Government was in the right. But to make the issue sure, he determined that in addition the rebellion should be put in 'the wrong.'"[130] Also, they state,

> President Lincoln in deciding the Sumter question had adopted a simple but effective policy. To use his own words, he determined to "send bread to Anderson"; if the rebels fired on that, they would not be able to convince the world that he had begun the civil war.[131]

Finally, these two secretaries concluded the Fort Sumter matter by stating,

---

[127]Tilley, *Lincoln Takes Command.*
[128]Ramsdell, "Lincoln and Fort Sumter," p. 285.
[129]Tilley, *Lincoln Takes Command,* p. 152.
[130]Ramsdell, "Lincoln and Fort Sumter," p. 286.
[131]Ibid.

When he finally gave the order that the fleet should sail, he was master of the situation . . . master if the rebels hesitated or repented, because they would thereby forfeit their prestige with the South; master if they persisted, for he would then command a united North.[132]

The best evidence, however, is contained in the diary of Lincoln's close and trusted friend, Senator Orville H. Browning. Senator Stephen A. Douglas from Illinois died after the war started, and on June 3, 1861, the Republican Governor, Richard Yates, appointed Browning to fill the vacancy. Browning had been a close personal friend of Lincoln for more than twenty years, and after becoming a senator he became a principal spokesman for the Lincoln administration. Lincoln had called Congress into session for July 4, 1861, but Senator Browning reported early and went to the White House to meet privately with his old friend on the night of July 3. Unknown to Lincoln, Browning kept a meticulous diary and he made an entry that night after returning to his hotel room about the discussion he just had with the president. The diary reports that after Lincoln read to Browning the message he was going to give Congress on July 4, he then put the document aside and Browning reports the conversation as follows:

He told me that the very first thing placed in his hands after his inauguration was a letter from Major Anderson announcing the impossibility of defending or relieving Sumter. That he called the cabinet together and consulted General Scott—that Scott concurred with Anderson, and the cabinet, with the exception of PM General Blair were for evacuating the Fort, and all the troubles and anxieties of his life had not equalled those which intervened between this time and the fall of Sumter. He himself conceived the idea, and proposed sending supplies, without an attempt to reinforce giving notice of the fact to Governor Pickens of S.C. *The plan succeeded. They attacked Sumter—it fell, and thus, did more service than it otherwise could.*[133]

---

[132]Ibid.

[133]Ibid., pp. 287–88; emphasis added.

If "the plan" was "to bring food to the starving garrison" then it failed. But if "the plan" was to provoke the South into firing the first shot, then it succeeded, and this is exactly what Lincoln stated.

Charles Ramsdell states that this diary entry "completes the evidence" that Lincoln provoked the South into firing the first shot, and Ramsdell explains Lincoln's conduct with Browning as follows:

> It is not difficult to understand how the usually secretive Lincoln, so long surrounded by strangers and criticized by many whom he had expected to be helpful, talking that night for the first time in many months to an old, loyal, and discreet friend, though a friend who had often been somewhat patronizing, for once forgot to be reticent. It must have been an emotional relief to him, with his pride over his consummate strategy bottled up within him for so long, to be able to impress his friend Browning with his success in meeting a perplexing and dangerous situation. He did not suspect that Browning would set it down in a diary.[134]

Rarely do historians find any better clue or "smoking gun" about a clever politician's hidden purpose than Browning's diary entry. On the next day, July 4, 1861, Lincoln gave his message to Congress and informed them that he had been trying to bring about a peaceful solution to the problem when he sent his ships merely to "deliver bread to a few brave and hungry men at Fort Sumter." He ended his message with these words, "And having thus chosen our course *without guile and with pure purpose*, let us renew our trust in God, and go forward without fear and with manly hearts."[135] Although Browning was a close friend and supporter of Lincoln, he must have blanched when he heard these words after having heard Lincoln's true story the night before.

There are many Lincoln supporters who maintain that Lincoln could never have used a trick to start a war because this

---

[134]Ibid., p. 288.

[135]Masters, *Lincoln, The Man*, p. 418; emphasis added.

would be out of character for a man who had expressed his anti-war opinions so strongly during his one term in Congress when he opposed President Polk's Mexican War. Lincoln charged Polk with provoking that war by ordering troops into a disputed boundary which caused the Mexicans to fire the first shots. One of Lincoln's most admiring historians has commented upon Lincoln's opposition to that war with the following comment:

> Politics of course also intertwined with Lincoln's moral revulsion to the Mexican War, as opposition to it became largely a party matter. Yet it is difficult to miss the fundamental anti-war meaning of his 1848 stand. He denounced the president of the United States, James K. Polk, for provoking the conflict: "The blood of this war, like the blood of Abel, is crying to Heaven against him." Lincoln made no apologies for attacking the commander in chief, for throughout history rulers [Lincoln said] "had always been . . . impoverishing their people in wars, pretending . . . that the good of the people was the object." This, he argued, was "the most oppressive of all Kingly oppressions." "Military glory," Lincoln defined as "that attractive rainbow, that rises in showers of blood—that serpent's eye, that charms to destroy."[136]

Gabor Boritt is obviously quoting, in part, from Lincoln's letter to his law partner, William H. Herndon, who had taken the position that Lincoln should not be criticizing President Polk for starting the war with Mexico and by tricking Congress into declaring war. Lincoln thought the war was unconstitutional because, in fact, President Polk had started it rather than submitting the question to Congress for a declaration of war. Lincoln's letter to Herndon stated that:

> The provision of the Constitution giving the war-making power to Congress, was dictated, as I understand it, by the following

---

[136]Boritt, "War Opponent and War President," in *Lincoln The War President: The Gettysburg Lectures*, Gabor S. Boritt, ed., pp. 190–91. Also, for a more full explanation of Lincoln's attack on President Polk, see Masters, *Lincoln, The Man*, pp. 97–98.

reasons. Kings had always been involving and impoverishing their people in wars, pretending generally, if not always, that the good of the people was the object. This, our Convention understood to be the most oppressive of all Kingly oppressions; and they resolved to so frame the Constitution that *no one man* should hold the power of bringing this oppression upon us. But your view destroys the whole matter, and places our President where kings have always stood.[137]

However, Lincoln learned many valuable lessons during his opposition to President Polk. He knew that Polk wanted the war in order to take property away from the Mexicans which they had refused to sell. He also knew that Polk could not afford to be perceived as the aggressor in starting the war. Lincoln learned from Polk that if you provoke the other side into firing the first shot and the American troops are thereby under fire, it is very difficult for Congress not to support the president and, therefore, to declare war, since to do otherwise would be a failure to support the troops in the field. He also learned that immense power and prestige immediately flowed to Polk as soon as the war began. Lincoln learned that once war is underway, all dissent from your opponents is stamped out, and the party in power is assisted greatly in getting its way with Congress. Lincoln also had endured much criticism for his attack on President Polk, and he had learned how unpopular it is to oppose a war in progress. The Democrats especially condemned him in 1848 for, "corruption" and "treason" of this new "Benedict Arnold."[138] Although most Whigs in Illinois agreed with Lincoln's opposition to Polk and accused the president of starting the war, one politician, who had been an opponent of the War of 1812, did not, and he explained that he would not oppose the Mexican War thusly: "No, by God, I opposed one war, and it ruined me, and henceforth, I am for *War, Pestilence,* and *Famine.*"[139]

---

[137]Mark E. Neelly, Jr., *The Fate of Liberty: Abraham Lincoln and Civil Liberties* (New York and Oxford: Oxford University Press, 1991), p. 213; emphasis in the original.

[138]Boritt, ed., "War Opponent and War President," p. 191.

[139]Ibid.; emphasis in the original.

Lincoln's Mexican War experience, far from proving that he would have been acting out of character by causing the Civil War, shows that he had an opportunity to learn many lessons which he could put into practice as president, especially for one who had less than 40 percent of the vote and minority representation in both Houses of Congress. With a war in progress, and the South not represented in Congress, the entire Republican agenda could be put into law. The South had always opposed the plan of the Federalist Party for a strong centralized government; the South had further opposed the Whigs, and now the South opposed Republicans, who stood for the same strong centralized government and also wanted a high protective tariff, internal improvements, as well as a partnership between big business and government.

Fareed Zakaria, managing editor of the influential magazine *Foreign Affairs*, is a great admirer of Lincoln's accomplishment in creating a strong centralized government, which changed America from a "backward" country to one that resembled the European powers. In his book, *From Wealth to Power*, he supports the fact that Lincoln was the first man to make America into a great war power, and he fully agrees with the change in foreign policy which finally occurred with the Spanish–American War and World War I. He concludes that a rich country like the U.S. should also be a "powerful country" through its military might, which helps it to expand its economic empire abroad. Zakaria describes the change of perception by European statesmen and especially Great Britain's Prime Minister Disraeli as a result of Lincoln's Civil War:

> European statesmen believed the Civil War represented a watershed from which there could be no turning back. Benjamin Disraeli explained in the House of Commons that the war would produce "a different America from that which was known to our fathers and even from that which this generation has had so much experience. It would be an America of armies, of diplomacy, of Rival States and maneuvering Cabinets, of frequent turbulence, and probably of frequent wars."[140]

---

[140]Fareed Zakaria, *From Wealth to Power: The Unusual Origins of America's World Role* (Princeton, N.J.: Princeton University Press, 1998), p. 48.

Very different ideas are contained in the correspondence after the Civil War between two prominent men, who both loved liberty and saw that a strong centralized government was a great threat to individual freedom and the whole concept of the American Republic created by our Founders. The great historian of liberty, Lord Acton, had been asked to write his opinions on the American Civil War, which he had followed very closely and had written about contemporaneously with the events. At the end of the war, he wrote to General Robert E. Lee, asking for Lee's opinions about the effect of the North's victory. In a letter dated November 4, 1866, Lord Acton lamented the defeat of the South and stated:

> I saw in State Rights the only availing check upon the absolutism of the sovereign will, and secession filled me with hope, not as the destruction but as the redemption of Democracy. . . . Therefore I deemed that you were fighting the battles of our liberty, our progress, and our civilization; and I mourn for the stake which was lost at Richmond more deeply than I rejoice over that which was saved at Waterloo.[141]

General Lee replied to Lord Acton in a letter dated December 15, 1866, and, in part, stated:

> I can only say that while I have considered the preservation of the constitutional power of the General Government to be the foundation of our peace and safety at home and abroad, I yet believe that the maintenance of the rights and authority reserved to the states and to the people, not only essential to the adjustment and balance of the general system, but the safeguard to the continuance of a free government. I consider it as the chief source of stability to our political system, *whereas the consolidation of the states into one vast republic, sure to be aggressive abroad and despotic at home, will be the certain precursor of that ruin which has overwhelmed all those that have preceded it.*[142]

---

[141]J. Rufus Fears, ed., *Essays in the History of Liberty, Selected Writings of Lord Acton* (Indianapolis, Ind: Liberty Fund, 1985), vol. 1, p. 363.

[142]Ibid., p. 365; emphasis added.

General Lee continued by stating:

> The South has contended only for the supremacy of the con-
> stitution, and the just administration of the laws made in pur-
> suance to it. Virginia to the last made great efforts to save the
> union, and urged harmony and compromise. Senator Douglass,
> in his remarks upon the compromise bill recommended by the
> committee of thirteen in 1861, stated that every member from
> the South, including Messrs. Toombs and Davis, expressed their
> willingness to accept the proposition of Senator Crittenden
> from Kentucky, as a final settlement of the controversy, if sus-
> tained by the republican party, and that the only difficulty in
> the way of an amicable adjustment was with the republican
> party. Who then is responsible for the war?[143]

Carl N. Degler, a Pulitzer Prize-winning historian, states that
most historians do not like to compare Lincoln with Bismarck of
Germany, but he shows that they were both men of "blood and
iron" and their achievements were very similar.[144] Both Lincoln
and Bismarck converted their respective governments, which
were both confederations of states, into consolidated *nations*.
Degler concludes that both needed wars to accomplish this feat.
Although Degler doesn't mention the welfare-state comparisons,
Bismarck was very explicit in creating the first modern welfare
state through the first social security system and the first work-
men's compensation act, while Lincoln's creation of the welfare
state in America was mainly corporate welfare, and then after the
war there were pensions for the veterans. Degler points out, however, that there is a very direct parallel in their respective cre-
ations of the warfare state.

One comparison leading to the warfare state which Degler
omits is that in the process of destroying confederacies to create
nations, both Bismarck and Lincoln became virtual dictators

---

[143]Ibid., p. 366.

[144]Carl N. Degler, "The United States and National Unification," in
Lincoln the War President: The Gettysburg Lectures, Gabor S. Boritt, ed. (New
York: Oxford University Press, 1992), p. 106.

essentially during the same period of time. Bismarck gained this distinction from 1862 to 1871 and Lincoln from 1861 to 1865.[145] Professor Forrest McDonald, in his excellent book surveying the American presidency, cites numerous sources, both by Lincoln's contemporaries and by current historians who all agree that Lincoln became a dictator:

> Many people, then and later, criticized Lincoln's conduct as excessive. The abolitionist Wendell Phillips called Lincoln an "unlimited despot," and Justice Benjamin R. Curtis wrote that he had established "a military despotism." When William Whiting, solicitor of the War Department, published a book called *War Powers under the Constitution,* in which he maintained that in wartime the president's actions are subject to no constitutional restraints whatever, Sen. Charles Sumner thundered that that doctrine (and Lincoln's behavior under it) was "a pretension so irrational and unconstitutional, so absurd and tyrannical" as to deserve no respect. The doctrine when followed changed the federal authority "from a government of law to that of a military dictator." Twentieth-century historians and political scientists routinely characterized Lincoln's presidency as a "dictatorship" or as a "constitutional dictatorship"—sometimes using the word in the benign Roman sense, sometimes in a sinister modern sense."[146]

Lincoln, as America's first dictator, brought some of the horrors of the French Revolution to our shores. He signed a warrant for the arrest of the chief justice of the Supreme Court because the judge rendered an opinion that Lincoln acted unconstitutionally by suspending the writ of *habeas corpus.* Lincoln persecuted Northern objectors to the war by having more than thirteen thousand people arrested without warrants, tried, and convicted in military courts unfairly and without due process of law, even though the civil courts were fully available for the trials.[147] After

---

[145]Randall, *Constitutional Problems Under Lincoln,* p. 57.

[146]Forrest McDonald, *The American Presidency* (Lawrence: University Press of Kansas, 1994), p. 400.

[147]Neally, Jr., *The Fate of Liberty,* pp. 10, 23.

the war, the U.S. Supreme Court, in the case of *Ex Parte Milligan* (1866) rendered one of its greatest decisions against presidential war power and in favor of individual rights by deciding that President Lincoln acted unconstitutionally by permitting the military trial of these civilians.

The government urged in the *Milligan* case that in the absence of restrictions imposed by Congress, the president is "sole judge of the exigencies, necessities, and duties of the occasion, their extent and duration," and that "during the war, his powers must be without limit." The Court unanimously disagreed, proclaiming,

> The Constitution of the United States is a law for rulers and people, equally in war and in peace. . . . No doctrine, involving more pernicious consequences, was ever invented by the wit of man than that any of its provisions can be suspended during any of the great exigencies of government.[148]

Lincoln had numerous members of the state legislature of Maryland arrested and placed in prison merely on the suspicion that they *might* vote for secession.[149] He also confiscated many railroads and more than three hundred "disloyal" newspapers. The supreme irony occurred when Lincoln had the grandson of the author of the *Star-Spangled Banner* arrested without a warrant and held in prison without any charges, merely on suspicion of disloyalty to Lincoln. This occurred at Fort McHenry, the very scene that had inspired the writing of the national anthem. Frank Key Howard wrote about this horrible experience in a book which was first published in 1881:

> When I looked out in the morning, I could not help being struck by an odd and not pleasant coincidence. On that day,

---

[148]Christopher N. May, *In the Name of War: Judicial Review and the War Powers Since 1918* (Cambridge, Mass.: Harvard University Press, 1989), p. 19.

[149]Bart Rhett Talbert, *Maryland: The South's First Casualty* (Berryville, Va.: Rockbridge, 1995), pp. 59–66; emphasis added.

forty-seven years before, my grandfather, Mr. F.S. Key, then a prisoner on a British ship, had witnessed the bombardment of Fort McHenry. When, on the following morning, the hostile fleet drew off, defeated, he wrote the song so long popular throughout the country, the "Star-spangled Banner." As I stood upon the very scene of that conflict, I could not but contrast my position with his, forty-seven years before. The flag which he had then so proudly hailed, I saw waving, at the same place, over the victims of as vulgar and brutal a despotism as modern times have witnessed.[150]

Secretary of State Seward basked in the power and the glory of the Lincoln dictatorship, even to the extent that he bragged to Lord Lyons, the British ambassador, "I can touch a bell on my right hand and order the arrest of a citizen of Ohio. I can touch the bell again and order the arrest of a citizen of New York. Can Queen Victoria do as much?"[151]

Degler points out that both Lincoln and Bismarck lived in a time when the trends were very different from today. While the approval of secession has been evident and was a very live issue during the last years of the twentieth century in Russia, Canada, Italy, France, Belgium, Britain, and even in the United States, Degler points out that between 1845 and 1870, there was much nation-building going on in the world. He gives six examples where there was either a failed secession or wars which brought about unification: (1) There was the revolt of Hungary against Austria which failed in 1848; (2) The Poles failed in a secession movement against Russia in 1863; (3) In 1847, the Swiss completed a Union under a new constitution modeled after that of America as a result of a civil war between the Catholic and Protestant cantons, which had caused a separation; (4) In 1860, Italy became united for the first time since Ancient Rome; (5) In

---

[150]John A. Marshall, *American Bastile: A History of the Illegal Arrests and Imprisonment of American Citizens in the Northern and Border States, on Account of Their Political Opinions, During the Late Civil War* (Wiggins, Miss.: Crown Rights, [1881] 1998), pp. 645–46.

[151]Masters, *Lincoln, The Man*, p. 411.

1870, Germany became united for the first time; and (6) Japan reorganized into a strong centralized government to replace the feudal society in the course of the Meiji Restoration.[152] Degler then analyzes the American Civil War, which he states is the best example of the unification process that was taking place at the time. He points out that under the original American Constitution there was a confederation of states, and America was not a nation in the "usual" or European sense. There had been many prior threats of disunion through the Kentucky–Virginia resolutions of nullification, the threat of New England states to secede after the Louisiana Purchase, the threat of New England states to secede after the War of 1812, and the South Carolina tariff nullification threat in 1832.[153]

Degler analyzes Bismarck's process of unification and states that he had to *provoke* two wars to create the German nation. Degler states that "all of the struggles for national unification in Europe, as in the United States, required military power to bring the nation into existence and to arm it with state power."[154] The German unification of its various states under Bismarck was not complete until the end of both wars. First, the Seven Weeks War was *provoked* by Bismarck on behalf of Prussia against Austria for the purpose of excluding Austria from Germany so that the militaristic state of Prussia would be the center and head of a future united Germany. By defeating Austria in 1866, he created a North German Confederation under the leadership of Prussia. Degler states: "Bismarck had provoked Austria into war to achieve his end."[155] The second step in the unification process was the Franco-Prussian War, which brought into the newly formed German nation the Catholic states of Bavaria, Württemberg, and Baden with Protestant Prussia, and the other Northern states.[156] Bismarck boasted in his memoirs that he *provoked* the war with

---

[152]Degler, "The United States and National Unification," pp. 92–93.

[153]Ibid., pp. 95–96.

[154]Ibid., p. 102.

[155]Ibid., p. 103.

[156]Ibid., pp. 107–08.

France by deliberately editing a report from the Prussian King, who was making a response to the French government. This has become known as the "Ems dispatch," and upon receipt of the reply, which greatly angered the French government, they declared war against Germany. Bismarck accomplished his purpose by committing the first act of aggression which provoked the French into declaring war, thus uniting all the German states into one nation under the leadership of Prussia and Bismarck himself.[157] He was in tune with Lincoln regarding the appearance of a defensive war in order to make it appear to be a "just war." Bismarck stated, "Success essentially depends upon the impression which the origination of the war makes upon us and others; it is important that we should be the party attacked."[158]

The foreign policy viewpoint of Great Britain, as seen through the eyes of its prime minister, Benjamin Disraeli, regarding the effect of the American Civil War has already been stated. It is interesting to compare here Disraeli's ideas about the newly unified Germany:

> As far as Germany was concerned, Disraeli's well-known remark in February, 1871 on "the German revolution" captured some of Europe's apprehensive reaction to the newly unified Germany. That revolution, Disraeli dramatically asserted, is "a greater political event than the French Revolution of the last century." He admitted that it was not as great a social event as the French upheaval, but "there is not a diplomatic tradition which has not been swept away. You have a new world. . . . The balance of power has been entirely destroyed, and the country which suffers most, and feels the effects of this great change most, is England."[159]

---

[157]Ibid., p. 108.

[158]Charles L.C. Minor, in M.D. Carter, *The Real Lincoln: From the Testimony of His Contemporaries* (4th ed., Harrisonburg, Va.: Sprinkle Publications, 1992), p. 256.

[159]Stig Forster and Gorg Nagler, eds., *On the Road to Total War: The American Civil War and the German Wars of Unification, 1861–1871* (Washington, D.C.: German Historical Institute and Cambridge University Press, 1997), p. 71.

The editors of the book *On the Road to Total War*, from which the above quotation was taken, reached the following conclusion:

> After all, in the making of nations, as Sherman advised, one must be prepared to use violence, even to the extreme of total war, if necessary. Abraham Lincoln, the lowly born democrat, and Otto von Bismarck, the aristocratic autocrat, could have agreed on that.[160]

Carl Degler, in commenting upon the American Civil War, stated that it "in short, was not a struggle to save a failed Union, but to create a nation that until then had not come into being."[161] Degler continues, "Lincoln then emerges as the true creator of American nationalism, rather than as the mere savior of the Union."[162] Degler's conclusion about the significance of the war is that:

> What the war represented, in the end, was the forceful incorporation of a recalcitrant South into a newly created nation. Indeed, that was exactly what abolitionist Wendell Phillips had feared at the outset. "A Union," he remarked in a public address in New York in 1860, "is made up of willing states."[163]

Degler also addresses the question of Lincoln's maneuvering the South into firing the first shot as follows:

> Over the years, the dispute among United States historians whether Lincoln maneuvered the South into firing the first shot of the Civil War, has not reached the negative interpretation that clings to Bismarck's Ems dispatch. Yet Lincoln's delay in settling the issue of Sumter undoubtedly exerted great pressure upon the Confederates to fire first. To that extent his actions display some of the earmarks of Bismarck's maneuvering in

---

[160]Ibid.

[161]Degler, "The United States and National Unification," p. 102.

[162]Ibid., p. 106.

[163]Ibid., p. 109.

1870. For at the same time Lincoln was holding off from sup-
plying Sumter he was firmly rejecting the advice of his chief
military advisor, Winfield Scott, that surrendering the fort was
better than provoking the Confederates into beginning a war.
*Lincoln's nationalism needed a war, but one that the other side would
begin.*[164]

In summary, Lincoln brought about the "American System"
envisioned by his hero Henry Clay, which included extremely
high tariffs to protect Northern industry from foreign competi-
tion, internal improvements for Northern business from tax rev-
enues collected primarily in the South, and a centralized federal
government strong enough to be "aggressive abroad and despotic
at home" as stated by Lee.[165] None of this could have been
achieved without destroying the American Republic created by
the Founding Fathers, and this could not have been done without
a war that excluded the South from Congress and then left this
region prostrate from 1865 until the middle of the twentieth century—a century which saw Lincoln's *nation* involved in two world
wars with the German *nation*, which Bismarck had created.

---

[164]Ibid., p. 108; emphasis added.

[165]See the excellent book by Frank Van der Linden, *Lincoln: The Road
to War* (Golden, Colo.: Fulcrum Publishing, 1998), p. 329, where the author
supports this general conclusion but fails to recognize the tariff issue which
caused Northern political and economic interests to demand a war to prevent Southern secession.

3

THE CALAMITY OF
WORLD WAR I

NIALL FERGUSON IS A history professor who taught at Cambridge and is now a tenured Oxford don. Those are the credentials of an establishment, or "court," historian, whose main purpose is to protect the patriotic and political myths of his government. Professor Ferguson,[1] however, has written an iconoclastic attack on one of the most venerable patriotic myths of the British, namely that the First World War was a great and necessary war in which the British performed the noble act of intervening to protect Belgian neutrality, French freedom, and the empires of both the French and British from the military aggression of the hated Hun. Politicians like Lloyd George and Churchill argued that the war was not only necessary, but inevitable.

Ferguson asks and answers ten specific questions about the First World War, one of the most important being whether the war, with its total of more than nine million casualties, was worth it. Not only does he answer in the negative, but concludes that the *world* war was not necessary or inevitable, but was instead the result of grossly erroneous decisions of British political leaders based on an improper perception of the "threat" to the British Empire posed by Germany. Ferguson regards it as "nothing less than the greatest *error* in modern history."

---

[1]Niall Ferguson, *The Pity of War* (London: Allen Lane, Penguin Press, 1998).

He goes further and puts most of the blame on the British because it was the British government that ultimately decided to turn the continental war into a world war. He argues that the British had no legal obligation to protect Belgium or France and that the German naval build-up did not really menace the British.

British political leaders, Ferguson maintains, should have realized that the Germans were mostly fearful of being surrounded by the growing Russian industrial and military might, as well as the large French army. He argues further that the Kaiser would have honored his pledge to London, offered on the eve of the war, to guarantee French and Belgian territorial integrity in exchange for Britain's neutrality.

Ferguson concludes that "Britain's decision to intervene was the result of secret planning by her generals and diplomats, which dated back to 1905" and was based on a misreading of German intentions, "which were imagined to be Napoleonic in scale." Political calculations also played their part in bringing on war. Ferguson notes that Foreign Minister Edward Grey provided the leadership that put Britain on the bellicose path.

Although a majority of the other ministers were hesitant, "In the end they agreed to support Grey, partly for fear of being turned out of office and letting in the Tories."

The First World War continues to disturb the British psyche today, much as the Civil War still haunts Americans. British casualties in the war numbered 723,000—more than twice the number suffered in World War II. The author writes that "The First World War remains the worst thing the people of my country have ever had to endure."

One of the most important costs of the war, which was prolonged by British and American participation, was the destruction of the Russian government. Ferguson contends that in the absence of British intervention, the most likely result would have been a quick German victory with some territorial concessions in the east, but no Bolshevik Revolution. There would have been no Lenin—and no Hitler either. "It was ultimately because of the war that both men were able to rise to establish barbaric despotisms which perpetrated still more mass murder."

Had the British stayed on the sidelines, Ferguson argues, their empire would still be strong and viable; instead, their participation and victory "effectively marked the end of British financial predominance in the world." He believes that the British could have easily coexisted with Germany, with which it had good relations before the war. But the British *victory* came at a price "far in excess of their gains" and "undid the first golden age of economic 'globalization'."

World War I also led to a great loss of individual liberty. "Wartime Britain . . . became by stages a kind of police state," Ferguson writes. Of course, liberty is always a casualty of war and the author compares the British situation with the draconian measures imposed in America by President Wilson. The suppression of free speech in America "made a mockery of the Allied powers' claim to be fighting for freedom."

While the book is addressed mainly to a British audience, it is relevant to Americans who tragically followed the British into both world wars at a tremendous cost in freedom as a result of the centralization of power in the leviathan government in Washington, D.C. There are many valuable lessons to be learned from this timely and important book.

4

FRANKLIN D. ROOSEVELT
AND THE FIRST SHOT

*The question was how we should maneuver them into the position of
firing the first shot without allowing too much danger to ourselves.*[1]

WORLD WAR II IS THE favorite war of modern liberals and neo-
conservatives who worship both a large, activist central government and an interventionist foreign policy. Part of the mythology
that surrounds this war is that it was the "last good war." It was a
"just" war because it was defensive. Despite President Roosevelt's
supreme efforts to keep America neutral regarding controversies
in Europe and Asia, the Japanese launched an *unprovoked surprise
attack* at Pearl Harbor, thereby "forcing" America into the fray. It
was also a "noble" war because America fought evil tyrannies
known as Nazism in Germany and fascism in Italy and Japan. The
fact that Stalin and Soviet Russia were our allies and that we
aided them with their oppression of millions of people during the
war and thereafter is ignored.[2] Finally, the advocates of the "last

---

[1]Quotation is from the diary of Secretary of War Henry Stimson
concerning the meeting with President Roosevelt and his cabinet on
November 25, 1941, just prior to the "surprise" attack at Pearl Harbor. See
George Morgenstern, *Pearl Harbor: The Story of the Secret War* (Old Greenwich, Conn.: Devin-Adair, 1947), p. 292.

[2]For the tyranny of Stalin and the Soviet Union generally, see R.J. Rummel, *Death by Government* (New Brunswick, N.J.: Transaction Publishers,

good war" say the Americans were generally united in their patriotic efforts to support the war. This helped to make us a great *nation* with a strong centralized government in Washington, D.C., which propelled America into an international leadership position as the world's policeman, thereby bringing "stability" to the world. World War II and the United States's participation have become patriotic myths to the American public, and all questioning of the official version of these events is discouraged, even viciously condemned, by the political, intellectual, and media establishment.[3]

I will argue, however, that President Roosevelt desperately wanted and sought a war. He not only provoked the Japanese into firing the first shot at Pearl Harbor, but he was ultimately responsible for withholding vital information from the Pearl Harbor military commanders which, if conveyed to them, probably would have prevented the surprise attack altogether.

Unlike the story in "Abraham Lincoln and the First Shot," where there was no official investigation of the Fort Sumter "incident," there were ten official investigations into the debacle at Pearl Harbor to see how such a tragedy could occur, killing nearly three thousand American servicemen, wounding thousands more, and causing massive damage to our Pacific Fleet. Many scholars, writers, and politicians who have studied the evidence gathered

---

1995) and his more recent book, *Power Kills: Democracy as a Method of Nonviolence* (New Brunswick, N.J.: Transaction Publishers, 1997). For American help to the Soviet Union during and after the war, see Werner Keller, *Are the Russians Ten Feet Tall?* Constantine FitzGibbon, trans. (London: Thames and Hudson, 1961), and also Major George R. Jordan (USAF), *From Major Jordan's Diaries* (New York: Harcourt, Brace, 1952). For British and American assistance to the tyranny of Stalin after the war, see Nicholas Bethell, *The Last Secret: The Delivery to Stalin of Over Two Million Russians by Britain and the United States* (New York: Basic Books, 1974).

[3]A classic example is the vicious smear tactics used against Pat Buchanan concerning his book, *A Republic, Not an Empire: Reclaiming America's Destiny* (Washington, D.C.: Regnery, 1999). See, for example, the articles about Buchanan and his book by Tucker Carlson, Robert G. Kaufman, and William Kristol in *The Weekly Standard* 5, no. 2 (September 27, 1999).

by these investigations have found, in fact, that President Roosevelt provoked the Japanese; that he withheld critical information from the commanders at Pearl Harbor; and that he misled the American people and Congress. Nevertheless, these Roosevelt admirers continue to defend and even praise him for his deceitful conduct. Typical of such apologists is Professor Thomas Bailey, a Stanford University historian of diplomatic relations, who declares.

> Franklin Roosevelt repeatedly deceived the American people during the period before Pearl Harbor. . . . If he was going to induce the people to move at all, he would have to trick them into acting for their best interests, or what he conceived to be their best interests. He was like the physician who must tell the patient lies for the patient's own good. . . . The country was overwhelmingly noninterventionist to the very day of Pearl Harbor and an overt attempt to lead the people into war would have resulted in certain failure and an almost certain ousting of Roosevelt in 1940, with a consequent defeat for his ultimate aims.[4]

The same Professor Bailey quotes Congresswoman Claire Booth Luce, who was also the wife of media mogul Henry Luce, as saying Roosevelt "lied us into war because he did not have the political courage to lead us into it."[5]

To address the defense of Roosevelt made by Professor Bailey requires a thorough discussion on allowing the president of the United States to become a virtual dictator, and that is not our focus. Bailey's defense of Roosevelt sacrifices all the safeguards provided by the Constitution and the democratic process, which

---

[4]Thomas A. Bailey, *The Man in the Street: The Impact of American Public Opinion on Foreign Policy* (New York: Macmillan, 1948), pp. 11–12; see also Bruce R. Bartlett, *Cover-Up: The Politics of Pearl Harbor, 1941–1946* (New Rochelle, N.Y.: Arlington House, 1978), p. 64.

[5]Thomas A. Bailey, *Presidential Greatness: The Image and the Man from George Washington to the Present* (New York: Appleman Century-Crofts, 1966), p. 155.

try to prevent the executive branch from having control over starting American wars. The Founding Fathers intended that only Congress should have the right to declare war and explicitly deprived the president of any war-making power in the Constitution. History, and especially English history, which was well-known by our Founders, clearly demonstrates that the king, or a few people in the executive branch, cannot be trusted with war-making powers.[6]

To study an event in history, such as the "surprise attack" at Pearl Harbor, it is necessary to study the ideas and events which preceded it, because history is like a seamless piece of cloth. The Pearl Harbor story is tied directly to British influence going back to World War I, and the British accomplishment of bringing America into that war. There are numerous books on the subject of this "surprise attack," but they differ in their conclusions on whether Roosevelt provoked the attack, whether he withheld information from the Pearl Harbor commanders, and whether Churchill and Roosevelt conspired to get America into the European war through the "back door" of a war first between America and Japan. However, all the books with which I am familiar on the subject of Pearl Harbor primarily examine the period of time from early 1939 through December 7, 1941. One cannot truly understand and appreciate the story of Pearl Harbor without seeing it as a part of the period starting in 1914, followed by America's entry into World War I and coming up through 1946 to the Pearl Harbor congressional investigations. World War II was actually a continuation of World War I and therefore, needs to be studied as one war which had a recess of twenty years, from 1919 to 1939.

Many people simply refuse to believe that President Roosevelt would conspire secretly with Winston Churchill to bring America into World War II by putting the Pacific Fleet at risk in Pearl Harbor to carry out this plan. If you only look at the period from 1939

---

[6]See John V. Denson, "War and American Freedom," in *The Costs of War: America's Pyrrhic Victories*, John V. Denson, ed., 2nd ed. (New Brunswick, N.J.: Transaction Publishers, 1999), pp. 1–11.

to 1941, you do not get the complete picture. The picture becomes clear only when you recognize the tremendously powerful political and economic forces at work in both the British Empire and America that caused Great Britain to enter World War I and then later got America into that war. Key British members of this same group, which has now become known as the Anglo-American Establishment, also practically wrote the Treaty of Versailles, which ended World War I. This unfair treaty led directly to the resumption of war in 1939 between Germany, France, and Great Britain which evolved into World War II. There are many events which Presidents Wilson and Roosevelt could not have brought about acting on their own to bring America into these two wars; but with both the public and secret participation of the powerful Anglo-American Establishment, America was dragged into these European wars against the wishes of the vast majority of American citizens. There is a well-established pattern by the Anglo-American group from World War I to Pearl Harbor, and the Pearl Harbor story fits into this pattern like a hand into a glove. In order to tell the Pearl Harbor story one must begin with World War I.

Another point needs to be made here. The "court historians"—or establishment journalists and historians whose main roles are to serve as both the progenitors and guardians of the political and patriotic myths of the nation, as well as protectors of the political leaders and special interest groups involved—accomplish their purpose by denigration and dismissal of any adverse explanation or exposure of these myths.[7] In most cases the court historians dismiss a refutation of the myth by simply stating that it is just another "conspiracy theory." They tend to explain most controversial historical events with their "lone nut" theory. While the court historians can't explain Pearl Harbor with the "lone nut" theory, they do dismiss the version related herein

---

[7]See Harry Elmer Barnes, "Revisionism and the Historical Blackout," in *Perpetual War for Perpetual Peace: A Critical Examination of the Foreign Policy of Franklin Delano Roosevelt and Its Aftermath*, Harry Elmer Barnes, ed. (New York: Greenwood Press, 1969), pp. 1–78.

as merely another "conspiracy theory." They also attempt to explain the Pearl Harbor story by stating that the very nature of the Japanese people is that they are treacherous and vicious and have a long history of "surprise attacks," which is really only a reference to their surprise attack on Port Arthur in their victory over Russia in 1905.

First, to tell the Pearl Harbor story, we need to recall the original ideas of our Founders regarding America's foreign policy—ideas which were completely repudiated in the twentieth century. The original American foreign policy which began with President George Washington and continued for one hundred years thereafter, is well stated in Washington's *Farewell Address* in 1797, which contained this prescient advice:

> Against the insidious wiles of foreign influence, (I conjure you to believe me fellow citizens) the jealousy of a free people ought to be *constantly* awake; since history and experience prove that foreign influence is one of the most baneful foes of Republican Government. . . .
>
> The Great rule of conduct for us, in regard to foreign Nations is in extending our commercial relations to have with them as little *political* connection as possible. . . .
>
> Europe has a set of primary interests, which to us have none, or a very remote relation. Hence she must be engaged in frequent controversies, the causes of which are essentially foreign to our concerns. Hence therefore it must be unwise in us to implicate ourselves, by artificial ties, in the ordinary vicissitudes of her politics, or the ordinary combinations and collisions of her friendships, or enmities.
>
> Why, by interweaving our destiny with that of any part of Europe, entangle our peace and prosperity in the toils of European Ambition, Rivalship, Interest, Humor or Caprice?
>
> 'Tis our true policy to steer clear of permanent Alliances, with any portion of the foreign world.[8]

---

[8]George Washington, *George Washington: A Collection*, W.B. Allen, ed. (Indianapolis, Ind.: Liberty Classics, 1988), pp. 524–25; emphasis in the original.

Murray Rothbard wrote a brilliant essay about American foreign policy and its change to interventionism at the end of the nineteenth century, expressly repudiating Washington's advice. This first put America at odds with the worldwide British Empire and its economic interests in our hemisphere in Venezuela over a boundary dispute:

> The great turning point of American foreign policy came in the early 1890s, during the second Cleveland administration. It was then that the U.S. turned sharply and permanently from a policy of peace and non-intervention to an aggressive program of economic and political expansion abroad. At the heart of the new policy were America's leading bankers, eager to use the country's growing economic strength to subsidize and force-feed export markets and investment outlets that they would finance, as well as to guarantee Third World government bonds. The major focus of aggressive expansion in the 1890s was Latin America, and the principal Enemy to be dislodged was Great Britain, which had dominated foreign investments in that vast region.[9]

The leading investment bank in America at that time was the House of J.P Morgan, which had tremendous influence over some members of the Cleveland administration, if not Cleveland himself. Rothbard continues:

> Long-time Morgan associate Richard Olney heeded the call, as Secretary of State from 1895 to 1897, setting the U.S. on the road to Empire. After leaving the State Department, he publicly summarized the policy he had pursued. The old isolationism heralded by George Washington's *Farewell Address* is over, he thundered. The time has now arrived, Olney declared, when "it behooves us to accept the commanding position . . . among the Power[s] of the earth." And, "the present crying need of our commercial interests," he added, "is more markets and larger markets" for American products, especially in Latin America.[10]

---

[9]Murray N. Rothbard, *Wall Street, Banks, and American Foreign Policy* (Burlingame, Calif.: Center for Libertarian Studies, 1995), p. 4.

[10]Ibid., p. 5.

This new foreign policy, which was announced, if not implemented, during the Cleveland administration, led directly to McKinley's Spanish-American War in 1898 and to America's acquisition of a foreign empire in Asia, thereby repudiating the traditional American foreign policy.

At the turn of the twentieth century, as America started its new interventionist foreign policy, the British Empire was the largest the world had ever known. The Industrial Revolution began in England, and, therefore, the British became the first nation to acquire all of the advantages of industrialization, including the creation of massive amounts of new wealth. A.J.P Taylor, a prominent British historian, comments on how Britain became and remained a great world power for more than three centuries:

> Though the object of being a Great Power is to be able to fight a great war, the only way of remaining a Great Power is not to fight one, or to fight it on a limited scale. This was the secret of Great Britain's greatness so long as she stuck to naval warfare and did not try to become a military power on the continental pattern.[11]

Through limited wars and military actions, the British had acquired numerous colonies throughout the world. It was perceived that these possessions were necessary for industrial development, to secure these colonies' natural resources and to provide markets for the manufactured products of the British economy. These basic factors of British and American political and economic development set the stage for World War I and America's entry into that war.

Neither World War I nor World War II were inevitable or necessary, especially from an American perspective; they were caused primarily by bad political choices that were greatly influenced by very large economic interests of a small number of politically powerful people. In fact, the entire twentieth century, in regard to the

---

[11]A.J.P. Taylor, *The Origins of the Second World War*, 2nd ed. (Greenwich, Conn.: Fawcett Publications, 1961), p. 284.

issues of war and peace, has been greatly influenced, if not controlled, by this Anglo-American group, which represents some of the world's most important economic interests. This group has supported the idea in America of a bipartisan foreign policy that causes little debate or discussion of the issues relating to foreign policy or to war and peace, and it has supported the concept of the "imperial presidency," which has given the president almost unlimited power over foreign policy. Arthur M. Schlesinger, Jr., in his book *The Imperial Presidency*, discusses the origins of the American bipartisan foreign policy, pointing out that it started when President Roosevelt put Republicans in his cabinet but that it became a dominant policy under President Truman. He points out that Senator Robert A. Taft strongly opposed both Roosevelt and Truman in this regard:

> "There are some who say that politics should stop at the water's edge," Senator Robert A. Taft had said in 1939. "I do not at all agree. . . . There is no principle of subjection to the Executive in foreign policy. Only Hitler or Stalin would assert that." Taft retained that belief after the war. In January 1951 he called the bipartisan foreign policy "a very dangerous fallacy threatening the very existence of the Nation."[12]

This Anglo-American group is not a dark, illegal conspiracy, although it does try to withhold its ultimate aims from public scrutiny. These people, or their minions, are openly active in American and British politics by holding elective offices and holding cabinet positions in their respective governments. Their financial contributions and political propaganda are immensely effective. They fully support the *private*-enterprise system, or *private* ownership of property and the means of production, but they strongly oppose the *free*-enterprise system advocated by Ludwig von Mises and the Austrian School of economics. The *free*-enterprise system proposes the complete separation of the economy

---

[12]Arthur M. Schlesinger, Jr., *The Imperial Presidency* (Boston: Houghton Mifflin, 1973), p. 129; see also the condemnation of the bipartisan foreign policy by Felix Morley in his excellent book, *The Foreign Policy of the United States* (New York: Alfred A. Knopf, 1951), pp. vi–vii.

from the government, whereas the *private*-enterprise system advocates a partnership between government and the economic interests involved, thus providing many economic and military benefits to businesses. This Anglo-American group has little difficulty
with a controlled economy. That is part of the price they pay for
this partnership, because they have such immense political influence that they actually use this governmental power to deter their
less politically-positioned competitors.

WORLD WAR I AND THE TREATY OF VERSAILLES
AS CAUSES OF WORLD WAR II

The Pearl Harbor "incident" brought America into World
War II, in 1941, two years after it had begun in Europe. In order
to understand why World War II *started* in Europe, it is necessary
to understand how World War I, in 1918–1919, *ended*. As stated
earlier, World War II was actually a continuation of World War I
in Europe, primarily because of the vindictive and fraudulent Versailles treaty that ended World War I. Prior to World War II, Germany attempted to revise the treaty peacefully and, after being
rebuffed by the Allies, decided to revise it forcibly. A.J.P. Taylor
has written the definitive work on the true origins of World War
II in Europe by cutting through the myths and false propaganda
presented by the Allies. He comments that:

> The second World war was, in large part, a repeat performance
> of the first. . . . Germany fought specifically in the second war
> to reverse the verdict of the first and to destroy the settlement
> which followed it. Her opponents fought, though less con-
> sciously, to defend that settlement. . . . If one asks the rather
> crude question, "what was the war about?" the answer for the
> first is: "to decide how Europe should be remade," but for the
> second merely: "to decide whether this remade Europe should
> continue." The first war explains the second and, in fact,
> caused it, in so far as one event causes another.[13]

Taylor goes on to explain how the peace treaty that ended
World War I was a major cause of World War II and concludes

---

[13]Taylor, *The Origins of the Second World War*, pp. 22–23.

that, "The peace of Versailles lacked moral validity from the start."[14] Therefore, in order to understand the causes of World War II in Europe, we need to take a brief look at World War I and why it was fought, as well as how it was concluded by this treaty.

The entry of Great Britain into World War I was greatly influenced by the same British political and economic interests who later joined with J.P. Morgan to bring America into World War I and World War II. The story of this Anglo-American group is told by Professor Carroll Quigley from Georgetown University, who has studied its organization and its tremendous influence on British and American foreign policy throughout the twentieth century. Quigley held positions at Harvard and Princeton prior to going to Georgetown University—where, incidentally, he had a student by the name of Bill Clinton. (President Clinton has stated that Professor Quigley was one of his favorite teachers at Georgetown.) Quigley wrote a book published in 1965 that discussed the Anglo-American group and its beginnings in England in the late nineteenth century:

There does exist, and has existed for a generation, an international Anglophile network. . . . I know of the operations of this network because I have studied it for twenty years and was permitted for two years, in the early 1960s, to examine its papers and secret records. I have no aversion to it or most of its aims and have, for much of my life, been close to it and to many of its instruments. I have objected, both in the past and recently, to a few of its policies (notably to its belief that England was an Atlantic rather than a European Power and must be allied, or even federated, with the United States and must remain isolated from Europe), but in general my chief difference of opinion is that it wishes to remain unknown, and I believe its role in history is significant enough to be known.[15]

Quigley explained that the group started in England under the leadership of Professor John Ruskin at Oxford University and

---

[14]Ibid., pp. 32, 277.

[15]Carroll Quigley, *Tragedy and Hope: A History of the World in Our Time* (New York: Macmillan, 1974), p. 950.

received most of its money from the imperialist Cecil Rhodes. The American contingent was consolidated initially around the House of J.P. Morgan, which helps explain Morgan's key role in getting America into World War I to help the British. He goes on to explain that,

> The original purpose of these groups was to seek to federate the English-speaking world along lines laid down by Cecil Rhodes (1853–1902) and William T. Stead (1849–1912), and the money for the organizational work came originally from the Rhodes Trust.[16]

Soon after Quigley published his book *Tragedy and Hope*, the publisher took the book out of print and destroyed the plates without consulting Quigley.[17] That is probably why his next book, *The Anglo American Establishment*, was much more critical of the group.[18] An accurate understanding of how and why the United States got into two world wars in the twentieth century to help the British Empire cannot be obtained without reading these two books by Quigley and Rothbard's *Wall Street, Banks, and American Foreign Policy*.

Quigley concludes his analysis of this Anglo-American group and its influence on world events with this sobering thought: "In foreign policy their actions almost destroyed Western civilization, or at least the European center of it."[19] Quigley also comments on the long-term significance of this group, especially the British portion thereof:

---

[16]Ibid.

[17]Popular American columnist Charley Reese from Orlando, Florida, confirmed this fact in a personal interview with Quigley's widow. Reese reported, "I verified this myself in a telephone interview with his widow. She said he had been extremely upset when he learned of it. He died not long afterward." (Charley Reese, *The Orlando Sentinel*, January 26, 1999).

[18]Carroll Quigley, *The Anglo-American Establishment: From Rhodes to Cliveden* (New York: Books in Focus, 1981).

[19]Ibid., p. 309.

[O]ne of the chief methods by which this Group works has been through propaganda. It plotted the Jameson Raid of 1895; it caused the Boer War of 1899–1902; it set up and controls the Rhodes Trust; it created the Union of South Africa in 1906–1910 . . . it was the chief influence in Lloyd George's war administration in 1917–1919 and dominated the British delegation to the Peace Conference of 1919; it had a great deal to do with the formation and management of the League of Nations and of the system of mandates; it founded the Royal Institute of International Affairs in 1919 and still controls it; it was one of the chief influences on British policy toward Ireland, Palestine, and India in the period 1917–1945; it was a very important influence on the policy of appeasement of Germany during the years 1920–1940; and it controlled and still controls, to a very considerable extent, the sources and the writing of the history of British Imperial and foreign policy since the Boer War.[20]

The British were the first modern nation to make imperialism into an "art of government," and they created their empire over several centuries by following three main aims: control of the sea, control of international banking, and control of the world's natural resources.[21] The foreign policy of the British Empire since the latter part of the sixteenth century has been to prevent the rise of any strong power on the continent, something they accomplished by forming various alliances to prevent any one power from achieving supremacy. However, with the consolidation of the German states under the leadership of Bismarck in the Franco-Prussian War of 1870–1871, an aggressive and economically powerful German nation burst forth. Thereafter, the British political and economic leadership perceived this new German *nation* as an extreme threat to their balance of power policy in Europe and to their dominance in the world, both economically and militarily.

Karl Helfferich, a prominent German banker and the finance minister during the war, commented in 1918 upon the economic

---

[20]Ibid., p. 5.

[21]F. William Engdahl, *A Century of War: Anglo-American Oil Politics and the New World Order* (Concord, Mass.: Paul and Company, 1993), pp. 8–19.

rivalry of Germany and the British Empire, as well as the reason the British declared war in August 1914:

> England's policy was always constructed against the politically and economically strongest Continental power. . . . Ever since Germany became the politically and economically strongest Continental power, did England feel threatened from Germany more than from any other land in its global economic position and its naval supremacy. Since that point, the English-German differences were unbridgeable, and susceptible to no agreement in any one single question.[22]

Helfferich sadly noted the accuracy of the declaration by Bismarck in 1897: "The only condition which could lead to improvement of German-English relations would be if we bridled our economic development, and this is not possible."[23]

American diplomat Henry White was instructed by his government in 1907 to meet with the appropriate British representatives in order to determine their views regarding the rising power of Germany. He met with Arthur James Balfour, who would later serve as the British foreign secretary during World War I and would become famous for the Balfour Declaration that led to the creation of the State of Israel in 1948. As reported by historian Allan Nevins, White's daughter overheard the following conversation at this meeting:

> Balfour (*somewhat lightly*): "We are probably fools not to find a reason for declaring war on Germany before she builds too many ships and takes away our trade."

> White: "You are a very high-minded man in private life. How can you possibly contemplate anything so politically immoral as provoking a war against a harmless nation which has as good a right to a navy as you have? If you wish to compete with German trade, work harder."

---

[22]Ibid., p. 38.
[23]Ibid.

Balfour: "That would mean lowering our standard of living. Perhaps it would be simpler for us to have a war."

White: "I am shocked that you of all men should enunciate such principles."

Balfour (again lightly): "Is it a question of right or wrong? Maybe it is just a question of keeping our supremacy."[24]

Also, by 1910, two of the new industrial powers, Germany and the United States, both had acquired strong centralized governments through their respective wars from 1861 through 1871, and this began to upset the "balance of power" in the world. Furthermore, Japan, with one of the world's oldest monarchies and a strong centralized government, became the only country in Asia that decided to industrialize, and it shocked the world by defeating Russia in 1905. Therefore, the British political leadership perceived that their world supremacy was threatened on the continent and in both the Atlantic and the Pacific regions. From an economic standpoint, America in 1910 moved into first place in the world of manufacturing output while Germany was second and Great Britain was third.[25] In addition, the rapid industrial progress that was taking place in America, Germany, Japan, and the British Empire had shown the extreme importance of oil. By 1912, the United States produced more than 63 percent of the world's petroleum, while England commanded no more than 12 percent of the oil production.[26] Germany and Japan, on the other hand, had no independent, secure supply of oil.[27]

Great Britain's balance-of-power policy, as applied by the British political leadership, viewed all these economic rivalries as a threat to its empire but saw Germany, which was the new strong

---

[24]Allan Nevins, *Henry White: Thirty Years of American Diplomacy* (New York: Harper and Brothers, 1930), pp. 257–58.

[25]Fareed Zakaria, *From Wealth to Power: The Unusual Origins of America's World Role* (Princeton, N.J.: Princeton University Press, 1998), p. 190.

[26]Engdahl, *A Century of War*, pp. 37 and 75.

[27]Ibid., p. 36.

man of Europe and which was only a short distance across the channel, as a far greater threat than either America, which was all the way across the Atlantic Ocean, or Japan in the Pacific. The author of *A Century of War* concludes in his analysis of World War I that:

> The British establishment had determined well before 1914 that war was the only course suitable to bring the European situation "under control." British interests dictated, according to their balance-of-power logic, a shift from her traditional "pro-Ottoman and anti-Russian" alliance strategy of the nineteenth century, to a "pro-Russian and anti-German" alliance strategy as early as the late 1890s."[28]

The British political and economic establishment did not expect the war to be as difficult or to last as long as it did and certainly did not think their "victory," with American help, would be as debilitating and costly as it turned out to be. A.J.P. Taylor explains that, "The first World War would obviously have had a different end if it had not been for American intervention: the Allies, to put it bluntly, would not have won."[29] He states further that, "The German army had been beaten in the field. It was in retreat. But it had not been routed or destroyed. The British and French armies, although victorious, were also near exhaustion."[30] Germany had not been invaded; in fact, its army still occupied foreign territory, and although it was in retreat, it could still fight. It was, obvious, however, that with American intervention, the eventual outcome of the war was certain to cause their defeat.

In the book, *The Pity of War*, British historian Niall Ferguson asserts that Great Britain should not have entered the European war (helping to make it a world war) and that the German government, under the Kaiser, was not truly a military or economic threat to the British Empire.[31] Ferguson concludes that if Britain

---

[28]Ibid., p. 38.

[29]Taylor, *The Origins of the Second World War*, p. viii.

[30]Ibid., p. 26.

[31]Niall Ferguson, *The Pity of War* (London: Allen Lane, Penguin Press, 1998).

had not entered the war, then America would not have entered, it would not have lasted so long, and it would have ended with a victory for the Kaiser's Germany. He points out that there were no binding legal ties with either Belgium or France to cause Great Britain to enter the war:

> Britain's decision to intervene was the result of secret planning by her generals and diplomats, which dated back to late 1905. . . . When the moment of decision came on 2 August 1914, it was by no means a foregone conclusion that Britain would intervene against Germany; the majority of ministers were hesitant, and in the end agreed to support [Foreign Secretary Sir Edward] Grey partly for fear of being turned out of office and letting in the Tories. It was a historic disaster.[32]

He further argues that, "[I]f a war had been fought, but without Britain and America, the victorious Germans might have created a version of the European Union, eight decades ahead of schedule," and the British would have remained strong, especially financially.[33] Ferguson then states that a short war won by the Kaiser's Germany would have produced a far different world for the remainder of the twentieth century, without Nazism in Germany or Communism in Russia:

> With the Kaiser triumphant, Adolph Hitler could have eked out his life as a mediocre postcard painter and a fulfilled old soldier in a German-dominated Central Europe about which he could have found little to complain. And Lenin could have carried on his splenetic scribbling in Zurich, forever waiting for capitalism to collapse—and forever disappointed. . . . It was ultimately because of the war that both men were able to rise to establish barbaric despotisms which perpetrated still more mass murder.[34]

---

[32]Ibid., p. 443.

[33]Ibid., pp. 458 and 460.

[34]Ibid., p. 460.

Ferguson closes his book by recognizing that World War I was horrible not only because of its destructiveness, but, more importantly, because it was avoidable, not inevitable. British leaders made a great error in judgment by taking Britain into the war, changing the whole course of the twentieth century:

> World War I was at once piteous, in the poet's sense, and "a pity." It was something worse than a tragedy, which is something we are taught by the theater to regard as ultimately unavoidable. It was nothing less than the greatest *error* of modern history.[35]

Murray Rothbard agrees with Ferguson's assessment of World War I and the great error made by Britain in entering that war, but he laments even more the great *error* that President Wilson made:

> American entry into World War I in April 1917 prevented [a] negotiated peace between warring powers, and drove the Allies forward into a peace of unconditional surrender and dismemberment, a peace which, as we have seen, set the stage for World War II. American entry thus cost countless lives on both sides, chaos and disruption throughout central and eastern Europe at war's end, and the consequent rise of Bolshevism, fascism, and Nazism to power in Europe. In this way, Woodrow Wilson's decision to enter the war may have been the single, most fateful action of the twentieth century, causing untold and unending misery and destruction. But Morgan profits were expanded and assured.[36]

Rothbard comments further about Morgan's direct financial interest in getting America into the war, which Morgan claimed was only to help the British:

> At the moment of great financial danger for the Morgans, the advent of World War I came as a godsend. Long connected to British, including Rothschild, financial interests, the Morgans

---

[35]Ibid., p. 462; emphasis in the original.

[36]Rothbard, *Wall Street, Banks, and American Foreign Policy*, pp. 20–21.

leaped into the fray, quickly securing the appointment, for J.P. Morgan and Company, of fiscal agent for the warring British and French governments, and monopoly underwriter for their war bonds in the Unites States. J.P. Morgan also became the fiscal agent for the Bank of England, the powerful English central bank. Not only that: the Morgans were heavily involved in financing American munitions and other firms exporting war material to Britain and France. J.P. Morgan and Company, moreover, became the central authority organizing and channelling war purchases for the two Allied nations.[37]

As we all know, hindsight is easier than foresight, but lessons should be learned from history; these lessons come by studying the political choices that were available and then by following the consequences of the choices that were made, as well as the probable consequences of the choices that were not made.[38] The British decided to enter the war for very poor reasons, mainly economic, and thought that, with the French and Russians, they could defeat the Germans quickly and conclusively. This did not turn out to be the case; therefore, the British desperately sought American intervention in order to crush the German economic and military "threat" completely. Even if the British had entered the war, but without American intervention, and regardless of who the victors were, a peace treaty would have been entered into much earlier and would have been concluded on much more equal terms, with the original German government—and probably the original Russian government—still in place. In this case also, the twentieth century would have been far different without Nazism ruling Germany and probably without Communism ruling Russia.

Colonel Edward Mandell House, President Woodrow Wilson's primary adviser, frequently visited England in 1914 and 1915 in order to discuss America's possible entry into the war. Finally, on October 17, 1915, and in spite of his political speeches calling for

---

[37]Ibid., pp. 15–16.

[38]See Niall Ferguson, ed., *Virtual History: Alternatives and Counterfactuals* (London: Papermac, [1977] 1997).

neutrality President Wilson wrote a secret letter to the leaders of the British government, offering to bring America into the war on the side of the Allies in order to cause them to win decisively. That would then allow Wilson to be the major player in dictating a permanent peace for the world.[39] House appealed to Wilson's insatiable ego by telling the president that he would be the "Savior of the World" and the new "Prince of Peace."[40] House praised Wilson's humanitarian motives for bringing America into the war, stating that he would play the "the noblest part that has ever come to a son of man."[41]

President Wilson was naïve enough to believe that the only war aims of the Allies (England, France, and Russia) were those stated publicly, "which included the restoration of Belgium, the return of Alsace-Lorraine to France, and the annexation of Constantinople by Russia."[42] However, one of the American delegates to the Paris Peace Conference that followed World War I was a knowledgeable diplomat by the name of William C. Bullitt. He later resigned his position as a delegate in protest of Wilson's actions at the peace conference, saying that Wilson did not understand the secret war aims of the Allies, and particularly those of the British, until the peace negotiations were all under way in regard to the Treaty of Versailles. Bullitt states the secret aims the British hoped to achieve at the peace conference:

[T]he destruction of the German Navy, the confiscation of the German merchant marine, the elimination of Germany as an economic rival, the extraction of all possible indemnities from Germany, the annexation of German East Africa and the Cameroons, the annexation of all German colonies in the Pacific south of the Equator . . . Palestine and as much of Syria as they might be able to get away from the French, the extension

---

[39]William C. Bullitt and Sigmund Freud, *Woodrow Wilson: A Psychological Study* (New Brunswick, N.J.: Transaction Publishers, [1967] 1999), pp. 170–71.

[40]Ibid., p. 170.

[41]Ibid.

[42]Ibid., p. 174.

of their sphere of influence in Persia, the recognition of their protectorates of Cyprus and Egypt.[43]

Bullitt then concludes that "All of these secret war aims of the British were actually achieved in one form or another by the Treaty of Versailles."[44]

The great classical-liberal American writer, Albert Jay Nock, commented on World War I and the Treaty of Versailles:

> The war immensely fortified a universal faith in violence; it set in motion endless adventures in imperialism, endless national- istic ambition. Every war does this to a degree roughly corre- sponding to its magnitude. *The final settlement at Versailles, there- fore, was a mere scramble for loot.*[45]

It was also during World War I that the British clearly rec- ognized how important, even critical, the abundant supply of oil was, not only for industrial purposes but also for military purposes. Therefore, one of their main economic and military aims was to help free the Arabs from the rule of the Turks (the Ottoman Empire) and then to take over the Arab oil interests after the war. The British used their agent "Lawrence of Arabia" to lead the Arab revolt against the Turks. Then, during the negotiations that led to the Treaty of Versailles, the British doubled-crossed the Arabs by grabbing their oil for themselves. By 1925 the British controlled a major part of the world's future supplies of petro- leum.[46] It was not until World War II that America, through the trickery of President Roosevelt, was able to grab "its share" of the Arabs' oil that the British had taken in World War I. William Eng- dahl states:

> They [the Rockefeller companies of the Standard Oil Group, together with the Pittsburgh Mellon family's Gulf Oil] had

---

[43]Ibid.,p. 173.

[44]Ibid.

[45]Albert Jay Nock, *The State of the Union: Essays in Social Criticism* (Indianapolis, Ind.: Liberty Press, 1991), p. 89; emphasis added.

[46]Engdahl, *A Century of War*, p. 75.

secured a major stake in concessions for oil in the Middle East, above all in Saudi Arabia. Partly through the clever diplomacy of President Roosevelt and the bungling of Britain's Winston Churchill, Saudi Arabia slipped from the British grip during the war. Saudi King Abdul Aziz gained an unprecedented Lend-Lease agreement in 1943 from Roosevelt, a gesture to ensure Saudi goodwill to American oil interests after the war.[47]

Engdahl also comments on the Versailles peace treaty and the League of Nations:

> Britain's creation of the League of Nations through the Versailles Peace Conference in 1919, became a vehicle to give a facade of international legitimacy to a naked imperial territory seizure. For the financial establishment of the City of London, the expenditure of hundreds of thousands of British lives in order to dominate future world economic development through raw materials control, especially of the new resource, oil, was a seemingly small price to pay.[48]

Engdahl further states that by 1919, after the signing of the Treaty of Versailles, the Persian Gulf became an "English lake."[49]

Murray Rothbard points out that the first formal joining of the Anglo-American group occurred at the Versailles peace conference in Paris when:

> [T]he British and U.S. historical staffs at Versailles took the occasion to found a permanent organization to agitate for an informally, if not formally, reconstituted Anglo-American Empire.
>
> The new group, the [Royal] Institute of International Affairs, was formed at a meeting at the Majestic Hotel in Paris on May 30, 1919.[50]

---

[47]Ibid., p. 102.

[48]Ibid., p. 50.

[49]Ibid., p. 51.

[50]Rothbard, *Wall Street, Banks, and American Foreign Policy*, pp. 25–26. The Americans created the Council on Foreign Relations in 1921 which coordinated their activities and policies with the Royal Institute.

Rothbard continues by revealing the heavy representation of the House of Morgan in this Anglo-American group. He also points out that the intense economic and political warfare between the Morgan and the Rockefeller interests, which began in the early years of the twentieth century, eventually ceased and that they joined forces to become the main leaders of the American portion of this group just before World War II.[51]

It is important to recall that, after World War I, a better informed and more realistic President Wilson admitted to the American people that World War I had not been an idealistic and humanitarian war to "make the world safe for democracy," nor had it been the "war to end all the wars." He toured the U.S. to try to influence public opinion to pressure the U.S. Senate to approve the Treaty of Versailles and to have the United States join the League of Nations, which the Senate wisely failed to do. Near the end of the tour, the discouraged president made a speech in St. Louis, Missouri, on September 5, 1919, wherein he abandoned his lofty statements and confessed to the American people what the real purpose of the war had been:

> Why, my fellow-citizens, is there any man here, or any woman—let me say, is there any child here, who does not know that the seed of war in the modern world is industrial and commercial rivalry? . . . This war, in its inception, was a commercial and industrial war. It was not a political war.[52]

---

[51]Ibid., pp. 27–37.

[52]Arthur S. Link, ed., *The Papers of Woodrow Wilson* (Princeton, N.J.: Princeton University Press, 1990), vol. 63, pp. 45–46. The Wilson administration discovered a silver lining in the cloud caused by the failure of the U.S. Senate to ratify the Versailles treaty, thereby leaving America technically at war until November 1921, when new treaties were signed proclaiming the end of the war. During this interim period, the Wilson administration pushed through legislation that still claimed to be part of the war effort. The Supreme Court, which traditionally had avoided judicial review of wartime measures, saw the danger, broke their long-standing rule, and began to judicially review these power-seeking measures. See Christopher N. May, *In the Name of War: Judicial Review and the War Power Since 1918* (Cambridge, Mass.: Harvard University Press, 1989).

The complete injustice of the Treaty of Versailles is a story that most British and American historians refuse to tell and one that very few of the American and British public know. In fact, the modern liberal line today, which is completely fallacious, is that World War II resulted mainly from the failure of the U.S. Senate to ratify the treaty and the failure of America to join the League of Nations. However, the true story of the Versailles treaty is very different and teaches an important lesson of history, as we shall see.

President Wilson, after injecting America into World War I, promised the Germans that a peace treaty would be effected with America as the leader of the conference and that the terms would be equitable and would not demand punitive war payments from Germany. The treaty, he promised, would allow self-determination for people throughout Europe so they could select their own governments. America, France, and the British entered into a pre-armistice agreement with Germany on November 5, 1918, with America and its Allies agreeing to make peace on the basis of President Wilson's famous Fourteen Points.[53] This promise proved to be fraudulent, and instead, a vindictive treaty was *forced* on Germany. A.J.P. Taylor describes the coercive measures, applied primarily by the British:

> There were other measures of coercion than the renewal of the war and occupation of German territory. These measures were economic—some form of the blockade which was believed to have contributed decisively to Germany's defeat. The blockade helped push the German government into accepting the peace treaty in June, 1919. . . . The negotiations between Germany and the Allies became a competition in blackmail, sensational episodes in a gangster film. The Allies, or some of them, threatened to choke Germany to death.[54]

After the signing of the formal armistice on November 11, 1918, the fighting stopped, but the British blockade of Germany

---

[53]Quigley, *The Anglo-American Establishment*, p. 237.
[54]Taylor, *The Origins of the Second World War*, p. 33.

continued, thereby causing the death by starvation of eight hundred thousand Germans, and resulting in a much-justified hatred of the Allies.[55] It was mainly the continuation of this naval blockade for six months after the war ended that forced the Germans into signing the unfair treaty.

The Treaty of Versailles divested Germany of its colonial possessions, allowing the British to expand their control in Africa to fulfill Cecil Rhodes's dream of an all-British route from Cairo to the Cape by taking the German colonies under the "mandate" in 1919. Most important, from a future political standpoint, it deprived Germany of any military defense by reducing the maximum number of its armed forces to only one hundred thousand men, which could hardly defend Germany from its traditionally hostile neighbors, especially the French and now *Soviet* Russia. The treaty prohibited Germany from having any airplanes, submarines, heavy artillery, or tanks. Germany had scuttled its own high-seas fleet under the waters of Scapa Flow to prevent its capture while the British retained the world's largest navy. The French, through the treaty, required the demilitarization of the Rhineland west of the bank of the Rhine which bordered on France, thereby keeping an open, undefended access to Germany's industrial heart in the Ruhr. France also maintained on Germany's border a great army, which was considered one of the world's finest.[56] In complete violation of Wilson's Fourteen Points, which called for self-determination, more than three million Germans were forcibly included in the country of Czechoslovakia and six million in Austria.[57] Furthermore, the treaty saddled Germany with the complete war guilt by branding her as the country that

---

[55]Charles Callan Tansill, "The United States and the Road to War in Europe," in *Perpetual War for Perpetual Peace: A Critical Examination of the Foreign Policy of Franklin Delano Roosevelt and its Aftermath,* Harry Elmer Barnes, ed. (New York: Greenwood Press, 1969), p. 96.

[56]J. Kenneth Brody, *The Avoidable War: Lord Cecil and the Policy of Principle—1933–1935* (New Brunswick, N.J.: Transaction Publishers, 1999), vol. 1, pp. 1–6, 99–123.

[57]Taylor, *The Origins of the Second World War,* pp. 146–81, 278.

started the war, a conclusion which she did not agree with or accept.[58] Another great injustice done to Germany in the treaty is the one that became the immediate cause of World War II. The treaty carved a wide path, or "corridor," through Germany from Poland to the German seaport city of Danzig, the strip of land that was taken from Germany in order to give Poland an outlet to the sea. The corridor completely separated East Prussia from the remainder of Germany, and the League of Nations took over the government of Danzig, declaring it a "Free City." Half a million German citizens within Danzig and the corridor suddenly became subject to the government of Poland, in complete violation of Wilson's promise of self-determination.[59] Finally, another great injustice was the creation of the huge debt for reparation payments or damages caused to the Allies, which was imposed on Germany in complete violation of Wilson's promises and the pre-armistice agreement. William Engdahl states:

> In May 1921, the Allied Reparations Committee met and drew up what was called the London Ultimatum, the "final" payments plan demanded of Germany. It fixed Germany's Reparations Debt to the victorious Allies at the astronomical sum of 132 billion gold Marks, an amount which even British reparations expert, John Maynard Keynes, said was more than 3 times the maximum which Germany could possibly pay.[60]

Taylor comments about the reparation payments, which lasted for thirteen years, from 1919 to 1932: "At the end the French felt swindled; and the Germans felt robbed. Reparations had kept the passions of war alive."[61] He comments further: "Reparations counted as a symbol. They created resentment, suspicion, and international hostility. More than anything else, they cleared the way for the second World war."[62]

---

[58]Ibid., p. 50; see also M.H. Cochran, *Germany Not Guilty in 1914* (Colorado Springs, Colo.: Ralph Myles, 1972).

[59]Taylor, *The Origins of the Second World War*, p. 189.

[60]Engdahl, *A Century of War*, p. 81.

[61]Taylor, *The Origins of the Second World War*, p. 47.

[62]Ibid p. 48.

Germany had been totally betrayed by America and the Allies in the peace negotiations. Delegate Bullitt commented upon the German reaction to the treaty:

> The Treaty of Versailles was delivered to the Germans on May 7, [1919]. The President of the National Assembly at Weimar, upon reading it, remarked, it is incomprehensible that a man who had promised the world a peace of justice, upon which a society of nations would be founded has been able to assist in framing this project dictated by hate. The first German official comment on the treaty was made on May 10, 1919. It stated that a first perusal of the treaty revealed that "on essential points the basis of the Peace of Right, agreed upon between the belligerents, has been abandoned," that some of the demands were such as "no nation could endure" and that "many of them could not possibly be carried out."[63]

Many of Wilson's advisers told him not to participate any further in the treaty negotiations and advised him to use his financial leverage over France and England to cause them not to enforce such a vindictive treaty against Germany. Wilson refused and continued to state publicly that he thought the treaty would be revised later by the League of Nations in order to make it fair.[64] Bullitt recounts that Wilson stated to Professor William E. Dodd later, "I ought not to have signed; but what could I do?" Bullitt then concludes, "He [Wilson] seems to have realized at times that the treaty was in truth a sentence of death for European civilization."[65]

William Bullitt resigned from the Paris Peace Conference and wrote a letter of resignation to President Wilson dated May 17, 1919, which contained the following statement:

> But our government has consented now to deliver the suffering peoples of the world to new oppressions, subjections, and dismemberments—*a new century of war*. And I can convince

---

[63]Bullitt and Freud, *Woodrow Wilson*, pp. 268–69.

[64]Ibid., pp. 261–63.

[65]Ibid., p. 294.

myself no longer that effective labor for "a new world order" is possible as a servant of this Government.[66]

Delegate Bullitt went on to state that this treaty would:

[M]ake new international conflicts certain. It is my conviction that the present League of Nations will be powerless to prevent these wars. . . . Therefore the duty of the Government of the United States to its own people and to mankind is to refuse to sign or ratify this unjust treaty, to refuse to guarantee its settlements by entering the League of Nations.[67]

The Treaty of Versailles was imposed on Germany's new government, again violating Wilson's promise of self-determination. This unpopular government, the Weimar Republic, was enforcing the treaty against Germany's interests, and was finally overthrown by Hitler's murderous Nazi movement, which won its power through the democratic and constitutional process with two main commitments: to fight communism and to end the unfair and vindictive treaty. Although the payments stopped in 1932, just before Hitler took office in 1933, the injustice of the payments had been a major part of his campaign. He continued to campaign against the remainder of the treaty after taking office and stated:

My programme was to abolish the Treaty of Versailles. . . . No human being has declared or recorded what he wanted more often than I. Again and again I wrote these words—the Abolition of the Treaty of Versailles.[68]

After gaining power, Hitler repeatedly petitioned the Allies to revise the treaty either to allow Germany to restore at least the equality of defense in military personnel and equipment with the other nations or to call for total disarmament by everyone. The

---

[66]Ibid., p. 271; emphasis added.

[67]Ibid., pp. 271–72; emphasis added.

[68]Alan Bullock, *Hitler, A Study in Tyranny* (New York: Harper and Row 1962), p. 315; also see Brody, *The Avoidable War*, p. 99.

Allies refused both offers.[69] Hitler then acted unilaterally to keep his promise to the German people by disregarding the treaty's limitations on Germany's defense and he rearmed Germany, first only to an adequate defensive position.

Hitler made one peace offer in 1936 that would have provided European security for the British and the French. He offered to agree that there would be no territorial claims in Europe, thereby accepting the German losses of territory in the treaty. He even proposed a twenty-five-year pact of nonaggression with all Western powers except Russia. Hitler had always maintained that the only war he wanted was with communism and Soviet Russia. In response to this peace offer, the British asked a few questions for further definitions but then refused to reply, and the French never replied at all.[70] A.J.P. Taylor comments on Hitler's foreign policy as follows:

> There was one element of system in Hitler's foreign policy, though it was not new. His outlook was "continental," as Stresemann's had been before him. Hitler did not attempt to revive the "World Policy" which Germany had pursued before 1914; he made no plans for a great battle-fleet; he did not parade a grievance over the lost colonies, except as a device for embarrassing the British; he was not even interested in the Middle East—hence his blindness to the great opportunity in 1940 after the defeat of France. . . . He did not wish to destroy the British Empire, nor even to deprive the French of Alsace and Lorraine. In return, he wanted the Allies to accept the verdict of January 1918; to abandon the artificial undoing of this verdict after November 1918; and to acknowledge that Germany had been victorious in the East. This was not a preposterous program. Many Englishmen, to say nothing of Milner and Smuts,[71] agreed with it even in 1918; many more did so later;

---

[69]Ibid., pp. 99–123.

[70]Taylor, *The Origins of the Second World War*, p. 100.

[71]Sir Alfred Milner was the key leader of the British portion of the Anglo-American Establishment, and Jan C. Smuts was an important member who was located in South Africa. Lord Robert Cecil was the leader of another bloc within the British portion of the Anglo-American group.

and most Frenchmen were coming round to the same out-
look.[72]

There has been much criticism of the Munich Pact as
appeasement, but Taylor comments:

> Only those who wanted Soviet Russia to take the place of Ger-
> many are entitled to condemn the "appeasers"; and I cannot
> understand how most of those who condemn them are now
> equally indignant at the inevitable result of their failure.[73]

Britain's reason for appeasement was primarily caused by the
sense of guilt on the part of the political and economic interests
identified by Rothbard and Quigley as the British portion of the
Anglo-American Establishment, because they were the principal
authors and beneficiaries of the unfair Versailles treaty. This
British group, usually called the Milner Group, negotiated the
treaty and virtually controlled British foreign policy during World
War I and thereafter. They were willing for Hitler to set aside
much of the treaty on a piecemeal basis, which would allow Germany to reclaim certain territory in Europe. However, the Milner
Group would not give up its economic gains received through the
treaty. These British leaders especially wanted Hitler to rearm to
a sufficient extent so that he could prevent Russian Communism
from taking over Europe, but they wanted it done unilaterally by
Hitler without their specific agreement, because that might reflect
badly on their "wisdom" in negotiating the original treaty.

The real irony of the beginning of World War II is that it
started over Danzig and the Polish Corridor question, which both
the British and French political leaders found to be the most inde-
fensible part of the treaty and one which most needed to be
revised peacefully. Hitler made numerous offers to the Allies and

---

However, Milner became the dominant member, and the group is often
referred to as "The Milner Group." See Quigley, *The Anglo-American Establishment*, pp. 15–32, 51–100.

[72]Taylor, *The Origins of the Second World War*, p. 71.

[73]Ibid., p. 292.

to Poland for settlement of the corridor question, one being to take Danzig back and let the people inside the corridor remain subjects of the Polish government. Another offer was to let the people within the corridor vote on which government they wanted. The British and the French, who were formal allies of Poland, pushed the Poles to accept these offers from Hitler.[74] Britain and France also requested that President Roosevelt push the Poles to accept Hitler's offers, but Roosevelt refused even to discuss the matter with Poland's representatives.[75] The Polish government arrogantly refused even to reply to these offers, and Hitler finally attacked Poland on September 1, 1939. Because of their treaty obligations, France and England then declared war against Germany on September 3 but refused to assist Poland in any way. Hitler had not expected the British and French to go to war over a treaty provision that they knew and declared to him to be completely unfair to Germany and to her people located in Danzig and the corridor. Taylor comments on this irony:

> In this curious way the French who had preached resistance to Germany for twenty years appeared to be dragged into war by the British who for twenty years preached conciliation. Both countries went to war for that part of the peace settlement which they had long regarded as least defensible. . . .
>
> Such were the origins of the second World war, or rather the war between the three Western Powers over the settlement of Versailles; a war which had been implicit since the moment when the first war ended. . . . Great Britain and France did nothing to help the Poles, and little to help themselves. The European struggle which began in 1918 when the German armistice delegates presented themselves before Foch in the railway-carriage at Rethondes, ended in 1940 when the French armistice delegates presented themselves before Hitler in the same carriage. There was a "new order" in Europe; it was dominated by Germany.[76]

---

[74]Ibid., pp. 239–68.

[75]Ibid., p. 262.

[76]Ibid., p. 267.

It is both ironic and noteworthy that Germany and Soviet Russia attacked Poland in September 1939, but that France and England only declared war against Germany while the Soviets became the allies of Britain and America thereafter. The final irony at the end of World War II was that Poland was not saved from tyranny at all but was simply transferred from German domination to that of Soviet Russia.

The French and British war on Germany was called "the phony war" because there was little activity on either side. However, in April and May of 1940, the Germans shocked the world by defeating the French in about thirty-five days of combat and drove an Allied army of 335,000 men, who were mostly British, to the beach at Dunkirk where they were hopelessly trapped.[77] Hitler gave orders to allow the helpless British army to escape in order to demonstrate dramatically that he had no quarrel with the British and desperately wanted to negotiate a treaty with them. He thought that a massacre at Dunkirk would inflame British public opinion and preclude a settlement with them. However, Winston Churchill became prime minister on May 10, 1940, and not only did he refuse to negotiate, but he immediately initiated bombing raids on German cities and civilians. War propaganda by the Allies, including America, has always stated that Hitler started the bombing of cities with his attack on the British city of Coventry, but the records now clearly indicate that Churchill initiated this.[78]

Taylor, the British historian, comments on this propaganda by stating that there was "almost universal belief that Hitler started the indiscriminate bombing of civilians, whereas it was started by the directors of British strategy as some of the more honest among them have boasted."[79] During the summer of 1940, after the bombing of civilians in German cities by the British, Hitler again

---

[77]See generally, Nicholas Harman, *Dunkirk: The Patriotic Myth* (New York: Simon and Schuster, 1980).

[78]James E. Spaight, *Bombing Vindicated* (London: G. Bles, 1944); Air Marshall Sir Arthur Harris, *Bomber Offensive* (London: Kimber, 1963).

[79]Taylor, *The Origins of the Second World War*, p. 284.

tried desperately to reach a settlement with Churchill but Churchill flatly refused to negotiate. It was not until November 1940, that Hitler retaliated by bombing British civilians and cities that were not military targets, such as Coventry.[80]

Therefore, we see that one of the main causes of World War II in Europe was the vindictive Versailles treaty and the failure of the Allies to revise it peacefully in the interim period between the wars. However, the Allies continued their parade of injustice at the Nuremberg war trials after World War II. One of the charges contained in count two was "crimes against peace," which was interpreted to mean that Germany had violated the Versailles peace treaty. The initial unfairness of the treaty was considered irrelevant and inadmissible testimony; this effectively prevented Germany from explaining any of her actions from 1919 to 1939, and prohibited her from showing the attempts to revise the treaty peacefully. At the trials, the Allies made it appear that Germany was simply an unprovoked aggressor against the peaceful powers of Europe, just as the war guilt clause of the Versailles treaty branded the Germans with sole responsibility for the outbreak of World War I.

None of this explanation for the cause of World War II should absolve Hitler for his murderous domestic policy. As Taylor points out, it was not Hitler's foreign policy that was evil; in fact, it was understandable and just, up to a point. Instead, it was Hitler's evil domestic policy, which resulted in the deaths of twenty-one million innocent unarmed men, women, and children killed during the war after Hitler had taken total control of the German government. Although Hitler achieved his office in a democratic and constitutional manner by promising to revise the Versailles treaty and oppose communism, after he obtained office, he went beyond Bismarck's consolidation of the states into a nation by *abolishing* all the states and creating a strong, totalitarian government. He finally declared himself dictator. As Taylor states:

---

[80]Ibid., pp. 284–87.

He changed most things in Germany. He destroyed political freedom and the rule of law; he transformed German economics and finance; he quarrelled with the Churches; he abolished the separate states and made Germany for the first time a united country. In one sphere alone he changed nothing. His foreign policy was that of his predecessors, of the professional diplomats at the foreign ministry, and indeed of virtually of all Germans. Hitler, too, wanted to free Germany from the restrictions of the peace treaty; to restore a great German army; and then make Germany the greatest power in Europe from her natural weight.[81]

Hitler's domestic policy however, was again proof of Lord Acton's famous phrase, "All power tends to corrupt; absolute power corrupts absolutely." There is no question that Hitler ranks as one of the most evil murderers in all history, but he still ranks third behind Soviet Russia's Stalin and Mao of Communist China. Stalin was personally responsible for more than forty-two million murders of innocent men, women, and children from 1929 to 1953, and the Soviet Empire itself ranks as the greatest political tyranny the world has ever known, with a total of sixty-two million murders of its own citizens from 1917 until 1987.[82] Mao ranks number two behind Stalin because as the Chinese dictator from 1923 to 1976, he murdered more than thirty-seven million of his own people.[83] One of the bizarre results of World War II was that it enhanced the two great Communist powers of Russia and China and destroyed the three most anticommunist governments: Germany, Japan, and Italy. World War II made the world much safer for communism and, thereby, more at risk to tyranny.

Finally, in regard to World War I and America's intervention, it is important to note that two of the key players in that war were also important figures in World War II. Franklin Roosevelt served in the Wilson administration as assistant secretary of Navy and

---

[81]Ibid., p. 70.

[82]R.J. Rummel, *Death by Government*, pp. 4, 8, 79–89.

[83]Ibid pp. 8, 91.

Winston Churchill played a much more significant role in the British government as the first lord of the Admiralty. Churchill's role in the *Lusitania* incident is remarkable, and this event became one of the major "reasons" Wilson used to bring America into World War I.

Just prior to World War I, the Cunard steamship company in England had received a government subsidy in order to build the *Lusitania* which was the world's fastest ocean liner. This subsidy allowed the government to participate in the design of the ship, which included a secret compartment where weapons and ammunition could be stored aboard ship. This subsidy further allowed the British government to take over full control of this ship during wartime. Colin Simpson, in his explosive 1972 best-seller *The Lusitania* gives the details of how the British, primarily through the actions of Churchill, used the sinking of the *Lusitania* to bring America into World War I to help defeat Germany.[84] When the *Lusitania* sank, more than one hundred Americans lost their lives.[85] On this fateful voyage, the British Admiralty, under Churchill's leadership, changed captains, substituting Captain William Turner for the usual captain. As the *Lusitania* drew near to its final destination, orders came from the British Admiralty to the military escort ship, the *Juno*, to abandon its usual mission, thereby leaving the ocean liner without protection from submarines. The *Lusitania* was not told that it was now alone, nor was it told that a German submarine was directly in its path—a fact known by the Admiralty. Finally the Admiralty ordered Captain Turner to reduce his speed, thereby making the *Lusitania* an easy target for torpedoes.

At the hearing held in England following this disaster, Captain Turner was made the scapegoat and found guilty of negligence, just as the American commanders at Pearl Harbor would later be made scapegoats for that disaster in World War II.

---

[84]Colin Simpson, *The Lusitania* (New York: Ballantine Books, 1974).

[85]William Stevenson, *A Man Called Intrepid: The Secret War* (New York: Ballantine Books, 1976), pp. 267–68.

World War II and British Influence
on American Foreign Policy Prior
to Pearl Harbor

Britain learned the hard way in World War I that it could not preserve and protect its empire without having the United States, with its economic and military strength, to help fight its wars to ultimate victory. The British openly sought American aid in advance of the European war that started in September 1939. On June 10, 1939, King George VI and his wife, Queen Mary, came to America and visited the Roosevelts at Hyde Park. According to King George's biographer, Roosevelt, in private conversations with the king, secretly promised the king full American support for the British Empire. Roosevelt agreed to set up a zone in the Atlantic to be patrolled by the U.S. Navy and the king's notes show that Roosevelt intended to sink German U-boats and await the consequences. The biographer of King George VI, John W. Wheeler-Bennett, concludes that these agreements served as the basis for the destroyer deal as well as for the Lend-Lease Agreement made much later.[86]

Another very important matter, related directly to secret conversations between Roosevelt and Churchill before America entered the war, is known as the "Tyler Kent Affair." Tyler Kent, a code clerk in the American Embassy in London, intercepted coded communications between Roosevelt and Churchill, who at that time was merely the first lord of the Admiralty. The code was supposed to be used only by the American Embassy in communications with the president and diplomats back in Washington. In other words, in violation of proper protocol, the president of the United States was not communicating with the head of the British government but was secretly negotiating with Churchill, who would not become prime minister for several months. Tyler

---

[86]See John W. Wheeler-Bennett, *King George VI: His Life and Reign* (New York: St. Martin's, 1958), pp. 390–92; also, see Ralph Raico, "Re-Thinking Churchill," in *The Costs of War: America's Pyrrhic Victories*, John V. Denson, ed., 2nd ed. (New Brunswick, N.J.: Transaction Publishers, 1999), p. 337.

Kent became concerned about the fact that these conversations revealed secret plans by which America was to be brought into the war in violation of the U.S. Constitution without a declaration of war by Congress. Scotland Yard learned that Kent had discussed these decoded messages with, and possibly showed them to, Captain Archibald Ramsay, who was a member of the British Parliament and known to be unsympathetic to the jingoistic Churchill.

Churchill became prime minister in May 1940 and immediately ordered the arrest of both Kent and Ramsay. The American government (Roosevelt) could have asserted diplomatic immunity for Kent and thereby prevented his trial but instead conspired with the British government (Churchill) to waive that immunity, and allow Kent to be tried secretly in a British court. Kent was found guilty of violating the British Official Secrets Act of 1911 and was placed in a British prison, where he remained for seven years and was not allowed to return to America until after World War II ended. Tyler Kent's information concerning the secret plans of Roosevelt and Churchill to bring America into the war, if revealed to the American people through a public trial in Britain, would have proved at least embarrassing to Roosevelt's administration and may even have led to his impeachment. Churchill also wanted the matter kept from the British people, therefore Ramsay, even though he was a member of Parliament, was held at Brixton Prison without any charges or a trial and was not released until September 1944. On the morning following his release from prison, he resumed his seat in the House of Commons and remained there until the end of that parliament.[87]

Another important matter to consider for the background of the Pearl Harbor story relates to a close personal friend of Winston Churchill, a Canadian citizen by the name of William Stephenson, who later became known by his code name, Intrepid. The full story of how Intrepid helped Churchill and Roosevelt drag America into World War II can be seen in three books: *A*

---

[87]See John Holland Snow, *The Case of Tyler Kent* (New Canaan, Conn.: The Long House, 1982); also, see David Irving, *Churchill's War: The Struggle for Power* (Western Australia: Veritas, 1987), vol. 1, pp. 193–96, 287–88.

Man Called Intrepid, *The Quiet Canadian*, and the very recent *Desperate Deception*.[88] One of Intrepid's agents was Ian Fleming, the author who popularized this secret British agency in novels and movies about James Bond.

Stephenson had made millions through the military-industrial complex of Great Britain during World War I, and it was at this time he became a close personal friend of Churchill. When Churchill became prime minister in May 1940, a year and a half before Pearl Harbor, he immediately arranged for financing from the royal family and, without any knowledge of Parliament, established a secret organization headed by Stephenson to be located rent-free in Rockefeller Center in New York.[89] Roosevelt had full knowledge of and was in agreement with this, but the U.S. Congress knew nothing of this deceitful action. The primary purpose of this organization was to help Roosevelt and Churchill bring America into the war through false propaganda, the creation of false documents, and whatever other means were necessary, apparently even including the murder of an American citizen who had established a supply of oil for Germany—a completely legal business relationship at the time.[90] Roosevelt stayed in constant contact with Intrepid primarily through an American lawyer by the name of Ernest Cuneo, whose code name was Crusader.[91]

Two false documents used by Intrepid were important in bringing America and Germany into the war against each other. First, Intrepid provided a false map that knowingly was used by Roosevelt in a national radio speech to the American people on October 27, 1941.[92] This document allegedly was obtained from a

[88]Stevenson, *A Man Called Intrepid*; H. Montgomery Hyde, *The Quiet Canadian: The Secret Service Story of Sir William Stephenson* (London: Hamish Hamilton, 1963); Thomas E. Mahl, *Desperate Deception: British Covert Operations in the United States, 1939–44* (Washington, D.C.: Brassey's, 1998).

[89]Stevenson, *A Man Called Intrepid*, pp. 30, 47

[90]Ibid., pp. 317–26.

[91]Mahl, *Desperate Deception*, pp. 47, 120, 193.

[92]Stevenson, *A Man Called Intrepid*, pp. 326–28; Mahl, *Desperate Deception*, pp. 55–56.

German spy and purported to show Hitler's secret plans for an invasion of South America, thereby demonstrating an imminent danger to America. Intrepid also created a false document that was put into Hitler's hands as an allegedly stolen secret plan of the American government.[93] It was received by Hitler on December 3, 1941, and purported to show Roosevelt's secret plans to make a preemptive strike against Germany without a declaration of war by the U.S. Congress. This document played a role in Hitler's decision to declare war against America on December 11, 1941, which surprised almost everyone except Roosevelt, Intrepid, and Churchill.

Intrepid also provided ammunition to attack Roosevelt's political enemies, such as Charles Lindbergh and Henry Ford, by creating false information that made it appear they were Nazi sympathizers.[94] Also, he launched a concerted effort that eventually destroyed the political career of a very distinguished Congressman, Hamilton Fish, who represented Roosevelt's district and who had opposed almost all of Roosevelt's foreign policy ideas on interventionism.[95] Intrepid exercised heavy influence over popular political writers like Dorothy Thompson, Walter Winchell, and Walter Lippman.[96]

It is important here to interrupt the story about Intrepid to discuss Lippman's views and the British group he worked with to influence America's entry into the war. The immense value of Walter Lippman to the British as a propagandist is clearly shown in David Gordon's excellent study of false war propaganda in general, and his case study of Lippman in particular.[97] Lippman argued that America should intervene in World War II because

---

[93]Stevenson, A Man Called Intrepid, pp. 326–34.

[94]Mahl, Desperate Deception, pp. 23, 34–35.

[95]Ibid., pp. 107–35.

[96]Ibid., pp. 47–68.

[97]David Gordon, "A Common Design: Propaganda and World War," in The Costs of War: America's Pyrrhic Victories, John V. Denson, ed., 2nd ed. (New Brunswick, N.J.: Transaction Publishers, 1999), pp. 301–19; see also Rothbard's account of Lippman's important role in Wall Street, Banks, and American Foreign Policy, pp. 19–20.

Germany was clearly a "menace" to the British Empire, and he concluded that since America's interests were "equated" with the British, Germany was equally a threat to America. Gordon points out that Lippman was the most influential American political commentator from 1930 through 1950 but that he did not manifest his real intentions until after World War II ended. In a short volume entitled *Isolation and Alliances*, which appeared in 1952, Lippman wrote about the American and British alliance:

> We were on the right course, as I see it, during the war—specifically, between 1942 and 1945. . . . During those years we had a close partnership, one might call it an organic alliance, which managed the business of war and peace in the Western world— managed it for what we have come to call the Atlantic Community.[98]

Lippman wanted a partial repeal or reversal of the American Revolution and the establishment of at least a permanent alliance with the British Empire. Gordon concludes that:

> Lippman, like Woodrow Wilson, had a hidden agenda. For this foremost columnist, the aim was not world government based on universal principles. Rather, it was a permanent union of the United States and Britain.[99]

Professor Carroll Quigley tells us that the British portion of the Anglo-American Establishment was very much in control of the intelligence and propaganda activities of the British government in America, with two of the British members of the Milner Group—Lord Lothian and Lord Halifax—serving as ambassadors to America. Quigley points out how significant this group was just prior to World War II:

---

[98]Quoted by Gordon in "A Common Design," pp. 318–19

[99]Ibid., p. 319; for a current statement on the idea of Great Britain merging with America as a full voting entity, see the article by popular British historian Paul Johnson, "Why Britain Should Join America," *Forbes* (April 5, 1999): 82–87.

Of even greater significance was the gathering of Milner Group members and their recruits in Washington. The Group had based most of their foreign policy since 1920 on the hope of "closer union" with the United States, and they realized that American intervention in the war was absolutely essential to insure a British victory. Accordingly, more than a dozen members of the Group were in Washington during the war, seeking to carry on this policy.[100]

Intrepid, who was obviously working for the Milner Group as a propaganda specialist, influenced Roosevelt even to the point that most of Roosevelt's important speeches on foreign policy were first cleared with Intrepid before they were actually given, so that the British agent could edit and revise them.[101] Also, Intrepid's agency became intimately involved in changing the results reached by Gallup polls.[102] Furthermore, Intrepid and his organization helped rig the Republican Party nomination for Wendell Willkie, whose foreign policy stance was almost identical to that of Roosevelt, thereby removing foreign policy as an issue in Roosevelt's bid for an unprecedented third term.[103] Intrepid's agency created false passes for a large number of Willkie supporters to come into the convention hall and chant for him throughout the convention, and they cut off the microphone for Herbert Hoover's speech.[104]

Intrepid's agency neutralized the opposition from Michigan Senator Arthur H. Vandenberg, who was a Republican and a staunch opponent of an interventionist foreign policy, thereby removing a strong potential threat to Roosevelt's reelection. The British provided three mistresses to Vandenberg, and then the senator's opposition to Roosevelt was compromised by the threat of disclosure.[105] Vandenberg later became a staunch interventionist

---

[100]Quigley, *The Anglo-American Establishment*, p. 303.
[101]Mahl, *Desperate Deception*, p. 58.
[102]Ibid., pp. 69–86.
[103]Ibid., pp. 155–76.
[104]Ibid., pp. 160–61
[105]Ibid., pp. 137–54.

and even helped President Harry Truman launch America into the cold war after World War II.

Intrepid followed the example first set by Sir William Wiseman, head of the British Secret Service in America during World War I, who had played a major role in getting the U.S. into that war. Wilson's adviser, Colonel House, "habitually permitted Sir William Wiseman . . . to sit in his private office in New York and read the most secret documents of the American Government. House's father and mother had both been English."[106]

Pearl Harbor

Now we turn to how America got into World War II at Pearl Harbor, events that propelled Franklin D. Roosevelt to "greatness." Roosevelt has always been ranked by "court historians" next to Lincoln as either the second or third greatest president in American history and this is due primarily to his involvement in World War II. Roosevelt struggled mightily to get America into the war by provoking "incidents" with both Germany and Japan, but it was the "surprise" attack at Pearl Harbor that finally did the trick. As will be shown, this attack was no surprise to Roosevelt and his key advisers in Washington. In fact, it was provoked by Roosevelt and his policies.

Background Specific to Pearl Harbor

In 1932, as a part of the annual maneuvers, it was documented by American naval planners that if there ever was a war with Japan, the Japanese would strike the Pacific Fleet wherever it was located. It was realized then that Pearl Harbor created a very vulnerable target for a surprise attack by aircraft carriers.[107] The studies revealed that, in order to prevent such an attack, a

---

[106]Bullitt and Freud, *Woodrow Wilson*, p. 160; see also Rothbard's account of the important role played by Wiseman in *Wall Street, Banks, and American Foreign Policy*, pp. 19–20.

[107]Morgenstern, *Pearl Harbor*, pp. 68–84; see also Bartlett, *Cover-Up*, pp. 52–53.

large contingent of American aircraft would be needed for a 360-degree surveillance, which would stretch out for long distances in order to provide sufficient warning to prevent disaster. The Japanese were very familiar with the findings of this naval maneuver in 1932; in fact, the Japanese patterned their attack of December 7, 1941, on the various studies done by the Americans concerning their own weaknesses.

In January 1940, Roosevelt ordered the Pacific Fleet transferred from its home base at San Diego to Pearl Harbor, with very little air cover or support.[108] On May 7, 1940, it was announced that the entire fleet would remain in Pearl Harbor indefinitely, which was a radical departure from American naval policy. Roosevelt further weakened the fleet by transferring many of its ships to the Atlantic to assist in delivering supplies and ammunition to the British and to try to provoke the Germans into firing the first shot against America.[109] Admiral James O. Richardson, commander of the Pacific Fleet, was so strongly opposed to these ridiculous orders that he made a personal visit to the White House to protest to Roosevelt, telling him that key naval officers were losing confidence in the president. As a result of this meeting, Roosevelt removed Richardson from command and replaced him with Admiral Husband E. Kimmel.[110]

The American people had become very disillusioned over being misled into World War I by President Wilson and were decidedly against entering another European war. Therefore, as Roosevelt sought to be elected to an unprecedented third term, he had to campaign for reelection as a peace candidate, as Wilson had before World War I. On September 11, 1940, Roosevelt stated, "We will not participate in foreign wars and we will not

---

[108]Morgenstern, *Pearl Harbor*, pp. 51–67.

[109]Ibid., p. 53; Bartlett, *Cover-Up*, pp. 29, 30.

[110]Morgenstern, *Pearl Harbor*, p. 63; Edward L. Beach, Captain, USN Ret., *Scapegoats: A Defense of Kimmel and Short at Pearl Harbor* (Annapolis, Md.: Naval Institute Press, 1995), p. 13; James O. Richardson, *On the Treadmill to Pearl Harbor: The Memoirs of Admiral James O. Richardson USN (Ret.) as told to Vice Admiral George C. Dyer, USN (Ret.)* (Washington, D.C.: Naval History Division, Department of Navy, 1973).

send our army, naval or air forces to fight in foreign lands outside of the Americas, *except in case of attack.*"[111] Later, on October 30 in Boston, he told American mothers and fathers, "Your boys are not going to be sent into any foreign wars. I have said this before but I shall say it again."[112] Two months after this promise, in early January 1941, he sent Harry Hopkins, his alter ego, to London to deliver a much different message. This secret message was just like the one President Wilson's alter ego, Colonel House, delivered to the British government on January 16, 1916, to promise American entry into World War I. Roosevelt made the same promise to the British. We now know through Churchill that on this visit, Hopkins reported to the prime minister the following:

> The president is determined that we shall win the war together. Make no mistake about it. He has sent me here to tell you that at all costs and by all means he will carry you through . . . *there is nothing that he will not do so far as he has the human power.*[113]

Later, Roosevelt and Churchill held a meeting, which became known as the Atlantic Conference, and released a statement in August 1941 called the Atlantic Charter. The British archives were opened on this subject in 1971, and soon thereafter, in January 1972, *The New York Times* reported that Churchill had told his war cabinet, upon his return from the Atlantic Conference with Roosevelt, the following statement which was recorded in the cabinet minutes:

> If he [Roosevelt] were to put the issue of peace and war to Congress, they would debate it for months. . . . The president had said he would wage war but not declare it, and that he would

---

[111]Benjamin Colby, *'Twas a Famous Victory: Deception and Propaganda in the War Against Germany* (New Rochelle, N.Y.: Arlington House, 1974), p. 21; emphasis added.

[112]Ibid.

[113]Winston Churchill, *The Second World War*, vol. 3: *The Grand Alliance* (Boston: Houghton Mifflin, 1950), p. 23; emphasis added; Colby, *'Twas a Famous Victory*, p. 22.

become more and more provocative. If the Germans did not like it, they could attack American forces.[114]

Churchill also reported that a decision had been made that the U.S. Navy would escort the British ships across the Atlantic, and the minutes of the British cabinet meeting contained these words from Churchill,

> The president's orders to these [United States Navy] escorts were to attack any [German] U-boat which showed itself, even if it was 200 or 300 miles away from the convoy. . . . *The president made it clear that he would look for an incident which would justify him in opening hostilities.*[115]

After America had actually entered the war, Churchill made a speech to the House of Commons on January 27, 1942, reflecting on the secret plans that he and Roosevelt had for America to come into the war, which is what they had discussed at the Atlantic Conference in August of 1941: "It has been the policy of the cabinet at almost all cost to avoid embroilment with Japan until we were sure that the United States would also be engaged."[116] Soon thereafter, on February 15, 1942, Churchill told the House of Commons:

> When I survey and compute the power of the United States and its vast resources and feel that they are now in it with us, with the British commonwealth of nations all together, however long it lasts, till death or victory, I cannot believe that there is any other fact in the whole world which can compare with that. This is what I dreamed of, aimed at, and worked for, and now it has come to pass.[117]

We now have the recollections of Churchill's son, Randolph, who relates that he had a conversation with his famous father before

---

[114]*New York Times*, January 2, 1972; Colby, *'Twas a Famous Victory*, p. 35.

[115]Colby, *'Twas a Famous Victory*, p. 36; emphasis added.

[116]Morgenstern, *Pearl Harbor*, p. 115.

[117]Ibid., p. 116.

America entered the war, and he asked his father how he was going to win the war. Churchill told his son, "I shall drag the United States in."[118]

One member of Churchill's war cabinet, Captain Oliver Lylleton, who was the British production minister, was well aware of the secret maneuverings of Churchill and Roosevelt to get America into the war, and he stated in a speech in London on June 20, 1944: "America provoked Japan to such an extent that the Japanese were forced to attack Pearl Harbor. It is a travesty on history ever to say that America was forced into war."[119] A member of the Roosevelt cabinet, Harold L. Ickes, stated, "For a long time I've believed our best entrance into the war would be [via] Japan . . . [which] will inevitably lead to war against Germany."[120]

In his excellent book on Pearl Harbor, George Morgenstern devotes an entire chapter to an analysis of the secret agreements made primarily between Churchill and Roosevelt before America entered the war. He also points out that the Dutch were included, mainly because of their oil resources in the Pacific. Roosevelt had secretly committed America to a war in the event the British and Dutch oil interests were put at risk by the Japanese, who desperately needed oil.[121] The military plan drawn up to carry this out, called "Rainbow Five," amounted to a commitment by Roosevelt to protect British, Dutch, and Chinese economic interests.[122] This secret agreement actually became public on December 6, 1941, but its significance was lost in the Pearl Harbor news the next day.[123] This secret agreement had been in place for eight months before Pearl Harbor, but it was never put into a formal treaty or even an executive agreement. It was simply an oral commitment by Roosevelt which had been committed into a definite written war plan for the Army and Navy. The plan had actually been

---

[118]Mahl, *Desperate Deception*, p. 1.

[119]Morgenstern, *Pearl Harbor*, p. 116.

[120]Beach, *Scapegoats*, p. 26.

[121]Morgenstern, *Pearl Harbor*, pp. 104–16.

[122]Ibid., p. 115.

[123]Ibid., p. 104.

approved in Washington by Secretary of Navy Frank Knox on May 28, 1941, and by Secretary of War Henry Stimson on June 2, 1941.[124]

Another close associate of Roosevelt and a frequent administration spokesman, Senator Claude Pepper of Florida (whose nickname was "Red" Pepper because of his leftist leanings), stated in an interview in Boston on November 24, 1941, that the United States was not far from a shooting war with Japan and that "we are only waiting for Japan to cross a line before we start shooting. I don't know exactly where that line is . . . and I am not sure the president knows exactly where it is, but when they cross it we'll start shooting." Pepper added that "actual declaration of war is a legal technicality and such technicalities are being held in abeyance as long as those brigands [the Japanese] continue in force."[125] Pepper was obviously aware to some extent of the "Rainbow Five" plan.

It was Secretary of War Stimson, however, who revealed after the war Roosevelt's secret wish of getting the Japanese to fire the first shot. In a statement to the congressional committee investigating the attack at Pearl Harbor, Stimson said, in looking back:

> If war did come, it was important, both from the point of view of unified support of our own people, as well as for the record of history, that we should not be placed in the position of firing the first shot, if this could be done without sacrificing our safety, but that Japan should appear in her true role as the real aggressor. . . . If there was to be war, moreover, we wanted the Japanese to commit the first overt act. [126]

Stimson's diary entry of November 25, 1941, thirteen days before Pearl Harbor, describes a meeting of the cabinet at the White House:

[124]Ibid., p. 109.
[125]Ibid., p. 290.
[126]Ibid., p. 292.

There the president . . . brought up entirely the relations with the Japanese. He brought up the event that we were likely to be attacked, perhaps [as soon as] next Monday, for the Japanese are notorious for making an attack without warning and the question was what we should do. *The question was how we should maneuver them into the position of firing the first shot without allowing too much danger to ourselves.*[127]

Provocations by Roosevelt

After the war had started in Europe in September 1939, but before America entered the war, Roosevelt committed numerous provocative acts in an attempt to create an incident that would involve America in the war to help the British.[128] One of the most provocative acts addressed to Germany was the Lend-Lease Act of March 1941, which was a virtual declaration of war. Roosevelt's action of sending fifty destroyers to England was clearly intended to provoke the Germans, and to aid the British.[129] In regard to provoking the Germans, one critic has stated:

Many have found Roosevelt's behavior on the eve of America's intervention in World War II especially reprehensible. Edward S. Corwin and Louis W. Koenig protested that, in the destroyer

---

[127]Ibid., emphasis in original.

[128]While Roosevelt claimed that the primary aim of America entering World War II was to defend the British from German "aggression," toward the end of the war, and during the wartime conferences—Yalta in particular—he seemed to have little concern for the British or for western Europe. At the wartime conferences, he was more concerned with his place in history and in achieving what his favorite president and idol Woodrow Wilson could not achieve; that is, creating a world organization with America playing a major role in it. Roosevelt repeatedly made concessions to Stalin in order to get Stalin's cooperation and agreement to form the United Nations wherein America and the Soviet Union would control the two largest spheres of influence. See also generally Amos Perlmutter, *FDR and Stalin: A Not So Grand Alliance, 1943–1944* (Columbia: University of Missouri Press, 1993), and Townsend Hoopes and Douglas Brinkley, *FDR and the Creation of the U.N.* (New Haven, Conn.: Yale University Press, 1997).

[129]Colby, *'Twas a Famous Victory*, p. 17.

deal, "what President Roosevelt did was to take over for the nonce Congress's power to dispose of property of the United States . . . and to repeal at least two statutes," while Senator William Fulbright accused Roosevelt of having "usurped the treaty power of the Senate" and of having "circumvented the war powers of the Congress." His detractors point out that six months before Pearl Harbor, on shaky statutory authority, the president used federal power to end strikes, most notably in sending troops to occupy the strike-bound North American Aviation plant in California; and that in the same period he dispatched American forces to occupy Iceland and Greenland, provided convoys of vessels carrying arms to Britain, and ordered U.S. destroyers to shoot Nazi U-boats on sight, all acts that infringed Congress's warmaking authority.[130]

Also unknown to the American people was the fact that Roosevelt put an American airplane with an American commander at the service of the British Admiralty to assist in tracking down the German warship *Bismarck*. Roosevelt commented to his speech writer, Robert Sherwood, that if it was found out he had done this, he would be impeached.[131] Roosevelt tried to use conflicts that he intentionally provoked between U.S. Navy ships and German submarines in the Atlantic as causes for America's entry into the war. On September 4, 1941, the USS *Greer*, was attacked by a German submarine off the coast of Iceland. The *Greer* had provoked the attack, but the president lied to the American people, stating that the ship was only carrying American mail to Iceland and was attacked without warning in international waters. The truth came out shortly thereafter when Admiral Harold Stark, chief of naval operations, disclosed that the *Greer* had actually been giving chase to the German submarine for more than three hours; the sub finally turned and fired two torpedoes at the *Greer*, which responded with depth charges.[132] Another incident is described as follows:

---

[130]Fred I. Greenstein, ed., *Leadership in the Modern Presidency* (Cambridge, Mass.: Harvard University Press, 1988), p. 35.

[131]Bartlett, *Cover-Up*, p. 9.

[132]Ibid., p. 29.

A few weeks later another American warship, the USS *Kearny*, was attacked and damaged by a German submarine. On October 27 the president told the country: "We have wished to avoid shooting. But the shooting has started. And history has recorded who fired the first shot. In the long run, however, all that will matter is who fired the last shot. America has been attacked."

When the truth of the *Kearny* incident finally came out, it became clear that Germany had not fired the first shot at all. Like the *Greer*, the *Kearny* had sighted the German sub and fired first. The result was that the American people refused to become inflamed by the incident. Thus when the first American ship, the USS *Reuben James*, was actually sunk on October 30, the president did not make much of it.[133]

These efforts to provoke the Germans into firing the first shot were unsuccessful because, more than anything else, Hitler wanted to avoid a war with America.

Roosevelt also tried to provoke the Japanese into firing the first shot, and eventually he was successful. An absolutely sensational book, and maybe the most important ever written on Roosevelt's role in the Pearl Harbor attack, was published in 2000.[134] The author, Robert Stinnett, a veteran of the Pacific war during World War II, devoted seventeen years to researching this subject. The book shows beyond any reasonable doubt that Roosevelt was directly involved in provoking the Japanese into firing the first shot at Pearl Harbor, that he was responsible for almost all of the critical military information being withheld from the Pearl Harbor commanders, and that he immediately launched a cover-up to make them the scapegoats while he pretended to be surprised and blameless. Stinnett states:

> By provoking the attack, Roosevelt accepted the terrible truth that America's military forces—including the Pacific Fleet and

---

[133]Ibid., pp. 29–30.

[134]Robert B. Stinnett, *Day of Deceit: The Truth about FDR and Pearl Harbor* (New York: The Free Press, 2000).

the civilian population in the Pacific—would sit squarely in harm's way, exposed to enormous risks. The commanders in Hawaii, Admiral Husband Kimmel and Lieutenant General Walter Short, were deprived of intelligence that might have made them more alert to the risk entailed in Roosevelt's policy, but they obeyed his direct order: "The United States desires that Japan commit the first overt act." More than 200,000 documents and interviews have led me to these conclusions. I am indebted to the Freedom of Information Act and its author, the late Congressman John Moss (D–Cal.) for making it possible for me to tell this story.[135]

Stinnett discovered the crucial document concerning Roosevelt's provocation in the personal files of Lieutenant Commander Arthur H. McCollum in 1995. The document reveals the eight-step plan Roosevelt used to cause the Japanese to fire the first shot. At Roosevelt's request, McCollum prepared the document, which is dated October 7, 1940, and McCollum and Roosevelt met at the White House immediately thereafter to discuss the same.[136] Stinnett relates how Roosevelt adopted the plan step by step. The plan set out the eight steps as follows:

A. Make an arrangement with Britain for the use of British bases in the Pacific, particularly Singapore;

B. Make an arrangement with Holland for the use of base facilities and acquisition of supplies in the Dutch East Indies;

C. Give all possible aid to the Chinese Government of Chiang Kai-shek;

D. Send a division of long-range heavy cruisers to the Orient, Philippines, or Singapore;

E. Send two divisions of submarines to the Orient;

F. Keep the main strength of the U.S. Fleet, now in the Pacific, in the vicinity of the Hawaiian Islands;

---

[135]Ibid., p. xiv.
[136]Ibid., pp. 6–10, 13–17, 28–29.

G. Insist that the Dutch refuse to grant Japanese demands for undue economic concessions, particularly oil; and

H. Completely embargo all U.S. trade with Japan, in collaboration with a similar embargo imposed by the British Empire.[137]

Lieutenant Commander McCollum commented at the end of the plan, "If by these means Japan could be led to commit an overt act of war, so much the better."[138]

The recurring theme in American history is that certain ships are offered by presidents as bait to get the enemy to fire the first shot.[139] Stinnett comments on this as follows:

Roosevelt's "fingerprints" can be found on each of McCollum's proposals. One of the most shocking was Action D, the deliberate deployment of American warships within or adjacent to the territorial waters of Japan. During secret White House meetings, Roosevelt personally took charge of Action D. He called the provocations "pop-up" cruises: "I just want them to keep popping up here and there and keep the Japs guessing. I don't mind losing one or two cruisers, but do not take a chance on losing five or six." Admiral Husband Kimmel, the Pacific Fleet commander, objected to the pop-up cruises, saying: "It is ill-advised and will result in war if we make this move."[140]

Admiral Kimmel was notified by the chief of naval operations on July 25, 1941, to be prepared to send a carrier-load of fighter planes to Russia which had been attacked by Germany in June 1941. Kimmel objected very strongly because he thought this would provoke the Japanese to fire the first shot and start a war and also because it would sacrifice a carrier and its airplanes. The idea finally was dropped.[141] Roosevelt also ordered separate suicide missions for three small ships based in the Philippines. With

---

[137]Ibid., p. 8.

[138]Ibid., p. 265.

[139]Lincoln, McKinley, Wilson, and Lyndon Johnson are good examples.

[140]Stinnett, *Day of Deceit*, p. 9

[141]Morgenstern, *Pearl Harbor*, p. 303.

American captains and Filipino crews, these vessels, each of which carried at least one gun, were to sail at different times toward Japan in an effort to draw Japanese fire, but the Japanese refused the bait.[142]

Roosevelt continued to follow the McCollum plan in all respects and, on July 25, 1941, he ordered all Japanese assets in the United States frozen, thus effectively ending all trade between the countries. This freezing order, in conjunction with an identical one from the British and Dutch, effectively cut off all oil from Japan that left them with approximately one year's supply in reserve at the time of Pearl Harbor and with no prospects for new supplies.[143]

The Japanese were aware that Roosevelt and Churchill were trying to provoke a war between America and Japan as a "backdoor" entry into the European war. Japanese Ambassador Nomura in Washington sent a coded message to Tokyo on August 16, 1941, two days after the announcement of the Roosevelt-Churchill Atlantic Charter Conference, which was decoded by the U.S. as follows: "I understand that the British believe that if they could only have a Japanese-American war started at the back door, there would be a good prospect of getting the United States to participate in the European war."[144] The Japanese, in an unprecedented diplomatic move following the Atlantic Conference between Roosevelt and Churchill, offered to send Prince Fumimaro Konoye, the prime minister, and a member of the royal family to America to negotiate personally with Roosevelt in a desperate effort to preserve peace. Roosevelt flatly refused such a meeting, thereby causing the downfall of the moderate, peace-seeking Konoye government, which was then replaced by Tojo's militant jingoistic government.[145] Furthermore, Roosevelt and

---

[142]Bartlett, *Cover-Up*, pp. 56–59; see also Kemp Tolley, *Cruise of the Lanikai: Incitement to War* (Annapolis, Md.: Naval Institute Press, 1973).

[143]Bartlett, *Cover-Up*, pp. 32, 38–39; and see Beach, *Scapegoats*, p. 28.

[144]Morgenstern, *Pearl Harbor*, p. 173.

[145]Bartlett, *Cover-Up*, pp. 39–41; also, see Morgenstern, *Pearl Harbor*, pp. 127–43. This refusal of Roosevelt to meet with the Japanese prime

Secretary of State Cordell Hull, in their negotiations with Japanese diplomats, presented ultimatums requiring Japan to get out of China completely, knowing that the Japanese would not accept those terms.[146] Japan was finally placed in the position of choosing either to lose the war without even fighting—basically because all of its oil supplies and essential war materials had been cut off—or gamble that a surprise attack at Pearl Harbor would cripple the American naval forces and cause America either to negotiate a peace treaty or to be so weakened that she would be unable to win a war in the Pacific.

Information Withheld by Roosevelt and Marshall

The extreme deceit of the Pearl Harbor attack is revealed further by the fact that Roosevelt and his key advisers in Washington had a tremendous amount of information that clearly pointed to Japan's intentions of launching a surprise attack at Pearl Harbor many days in advance and with plenty of time to either prevent the same or prepare for the event, but they withheld most of it from the Pearl Harbor commanders. Both Admiral Husband E. Kimmel and Lieutenant General Walter C. Short, the military commanders at Pearl Harbor, had been promised in writing by their respective chiefs of service that all information pertaining to their posts, regardless of the source of the information, would be delivered immediately from Washington to them directly. In fact, Admiral Kimmel made a special trip to Washington in June 1941

---

minister is very much like Lincoln's refusal to meet and discuss peace terms with the Confederate commissioners, with very similar results in regard to preserving the peace.

[146]Beach, *Scapegoats*, p. 32. A.J.P. Taylor states that Manchuria received "mythical importance" and was "treated as a milestone on the road to war," when, in fact, the commission designated by the League of Nations investigated the Manchurian incident at the initiative of the Japanese and found that the Japanese grievances were justified and Japan was not condemned as an aggressor, although Japan was condemned for resorting to force before all peaceful means had been exhausted. Taylor states, "The Chinese reconciled themselves to the loss of a province which they had not controlled for some years; and in 1933 peace was restored between China and Japan." See Taylor, *The Origins of the Second World War*, p. 65.

to meet with Admiral Harold R. Stark, chief of naval operations, requesting this pledge to get the information. Stark, in turn, gave his absolute assurance that all information would be passed along.[147]

On January 27, 1941, the American ambassador to Japan, Joseph Grew, sent the following dispatch to Washington:

> My Peruvian colleague told a member of my staff that he had heard from many sources including a Japanese source that the Japanese military forces planned, in the event of trouble with the United States, to attempt a surprise mass attack on Pearl Harbor using all of their military facilities. He added that although the project seemed fantastic the fact that he had heard it from many sources prompted him to pass on the information.[148]

Admiral Stark relayed this information to Admiral Kimmel but reported that it was only a rumor and that he should put no stock in it.[149] The fact that "a rumor" was reported clearly led Admiral Kimmel to believe he was receiving all the information available to his superiors in Washington.

Prior to Stinnett's book, it was known that certain Japanese spies were sending messages to Japan stating the location and activity of the ships in Pearl Harbor. Also, it was known that American cryptographers had solved the purple, or diplomatic, code of the Japanese. However, the critical information about the attack was in the naval or military code of the Japanese, and Stinnett discovered these secret messages that were known to Roosevelt and withheld from the Pearl Harbor commanders and the American public for more than fifty years. Stinnett states "The truth of Pearl Harbor is found in the Naval Codes, not in the diplomatic codes."[150] The American cryptographers broke the naval or military code of the Japanese in October 1940.[151]

---

[147]Beach, *Scapegoats*, p. 11.

[148]Bartlett, *Cover-Up*, p. 53.

[149]Beach, *Scapegoats*, p. 48.

[150]Stinnett, *Day of Deceit*, p. 21.

[151]Ibid., p. 22.

Some of the most startling revelations made by Stinnett show that, contrary to prior assertions made in sworn testimony at congressional hearings, the Japanese fleet that set out for Pearl Harbor on November 25, 1941, did *not* maintain radio silence up through December 7, 1941. In fact, American cryptographers were decoding the military communications and sending them directly to Roosevelt; through directional radio finders, they were able to determine the exact location of the fleet all the way through their fateful journey. Roosevelt ordered all ships out of the North Pacific Ocean when he learned that the Japanese forces were in that area, and he did this to prevent any discovery of the Japanese presence there. Stinnett reports:

> Navy officials declared the North Pacific Ocean a "Vacant Sea" and ordered all U.S. and allied shipping out of the waters. An alternate trans-Pacific route was authorized through the Torrens Strait, in the South Pacific between Australia and New Guinea. Rear Admiral Richmond K. Turner, War Plans officer for the United States Navy in 1941, explained the reasoning with a startling admission: "We were prepared to divert traffic when we believed that war was imminent. We sent the traffic down via Torrens Strait, so that the track of the Japanese task force would be clear of any traffic." On November 25, the day that the Japanese carrier force sailed for Pearl Harbor, Navy headquarters sent this message to Kimmel and San Francisco's Twelfth Naval District:
>
> ROUTE ALL TRANSPACIFIC SHIPPING THRU TORRENS STRAITS. CINCPAC AND CINCAF PROVIDE NECESSARY ESCORT REFER YOUR DISPATCH 230258.
>
> The order was dispatched about an hour after Admiral Nagumo's carrier force departed Hitokappu Bay and entered the North Pacific.
>
> The "vacant sea" order dramatizes Admiral Kimmel's helplessness in the face of Roosevelt's desires. The admiral tried on a number of occasions to do something to defend Pearl Harbor, based on Rochefort's troubling intercepts. Exactly two weeks prior to the attack, Kimmel ordered a search for a Japanese carrier force north of Hawaii. Without White House approval, he moved the Pacific Fleet into the North Pacific Ocean in the precise area where Japan planned to launch her

carrier attack on Pearl Harbor. But his laudable efforts came to naught. When White House military officials learned Kimmel's warships were in the area of what turned out to be the intended Japanese launch site, they issued directives that caused Kimmel to quickly order the Pacific Fleet out of the North Pacific and back to its anchorages in Pearl Harbor.[152]

Stinnett reports further that:

> At the time, of course, Kimmel did not know of Washington's eight-action policy. If McCollum's action policy was to succeed in uniting America, Japan must be seen as the aggressor and must commit the first overt act of war on an unsuspecting Pacific Fleet, not the other way around. FDR and his highest-level commanders gambled on Japan committing the first overt act of war, and knew from intercepted messages that it was near. An open sea engagement between Japan's carrier force and the Pacific Fleet would have been far less effective at establishing American outrage. Japan could claim that its right to sail the open seas had been deliberately challenged by American warships if Kimmel attacked first.[153]

Stinnett further shows how Roosevelt ordered Kimmel's ships around like they were on strings:

> On orders from Washington, Kimmel left his oldest vessels inside Pearl Harbor and sent twenty-one modern warships, including his two aircraft carriers, west toward Wake and Midway. Those were strange orders, for they dispatched American forces directly into the path of the oncoming Japanese fleet of thirty submarines. The last-minute circumstances that moved the warships out of Pearl Harbor were discussed during the 1945–46 Congressional inquiry. Members wondered whether the sorties were genuine efforts to reinforce Wake Island and Midway or merely ploys to move all the modern warships from the Pearl Harbor anchorages prior to the attack so they would not be hit by the First Air Fleet. . . . With the departure of the Lexington and Enterprise groups, the warships remaining in

---

[152]Ibid., pp. 144–45.
[153]Ibid., p. 151.

Pearl Harbor were mostly twenty-seven-year-old relics of World War I.[154]

Prior to Stinnett's book, a British code-breaker published a book entitled *Betrayal at Pearl Harbor*.[155] This sensational book states that on or about November 25, 1941, the British were able to overhear the Japanese military commands relating to a large military operation, including aircraft carriers, battleships, and other vessels that were leaving Japanese waters headed to Hawaii. The book's co-author, Captain Eric Nave, personally passed this information—which clearly indicated the Japanese were headed for a surprise attack at Pearl Harbor—directly to Churchill. The book is inconclusive, however, as to whether Churchill actually relayed this message to Roosevelt.[156] Prior to the Stinnett book, a book by former CIA director William Casey, entitled *The Secret War Against Hitler*, states:

> As the Japanese storm began to gather force in the Pacific, the most private communications between the Japanese government and its ambassadors . . . were being read in Washington. Army and Navy cryptographers having broken the Japanese

---

[154]Ibid., pp. 152 and 154.

[155]James Rusbridger and Eric Nave, *Betrayal at Pearl Harbor: How Churchill Lured Roosevelt into World War II* (New York: Summit Books, 1991).

[156]Another sensational book describes and quotes verbatim the alleged intercepted radio communications between Churchill and Roosevelt concerning the essential message that the Japanese were headed to Pearl Harbor for a surprise attack. There is a series of books relating to alleged interviews by an American CIA agent with Heinrich Müller, who was the Gestapo chief under Hitler. These interviews with Müller allegedly took place at the end of the war; and Müller states that the Germans were able to intercept the radio communications between Roosevelt and Churchill because the Germans had the identical communications system. The German interception of these comments between Churchill and Roosevelt shows that Churchill gave explicit information to Roosevelt that the Japanese were headed to Pearl Harbor for a surprise attack. See Gregory Douglas, *Gestapo Chief: The 1948 Interrogation of Heinrich Müller* (San Jose, Calif.: R. James Bender, 1998), vol. 3, pp. 48–99.

diplomatic cipher, were reading messages that foretold the attack. *The British had sent word that a Japanese fleet was steaming east toward Hawaii.*[157]

Some of the most important information that was *never* passed along to Kimmel and Short and was never even available to them to use in their own defense were the "bomb plot" messages of September 24, 1941, and thereafter.[158] Japanese spies in Hawaii regularly were reporting the positions of all ships in Pearl Harbor and this information drastically increased the week before the attack, even including information that ships were not moved. A grid system was set up so that they could tell the position of the ships within that system—a clear indication that an air attack was a strong probability.[159]

Admiral Kimmel, in his own book that was published before it was known that the Japanese military orders had been intercepted, stated that key information was withheld from him and that he thought the bomb plot messages were probably the most essential pieces of military information that should have been communicated to him:

> The deficiencies of Pearl Harbor as a fleet base were well known in the Navy Department. In an interview with Mr. Roosevelt in June 1941, in Washington, I outlined the weaknesses and concluded with the remark that the only answer was to have the fleet at sea if the Japs ever attacked.
>
> I accepted the decision to base the fleet at Pearl Harbor in the firm belief that the Navy Department would supply me promptly with all pertinent information available and in particular with all information that indicated an attack on the fleet at Pearl Harbor. . . .
>
> The care taken to keep the commander-in-chief of our Asiatic Fleet and the British in London informed of Japanese

---

[157]William Casey, *The Secret War Against Hitler* (Washington, D.C.: Regnery Gateway, 1988), p. 7; emphasis added.

[158]Beach, *Scapegoats*, p. 34.

[159]Ibid., pp. 35–36, 92.

intentions while withholding this vital information from our commanders at Pearl Harbor has never been explained.

The Navy Department thus engaged in a course of conduct which definitely gave me the impression that intelligence from important intercepted Japanese messages was being furnished to me. Under these circumstances a failure to send me important information of this character was not merely withholding of intelligence. *It amounted to an affirmative misrepresentation.* I had asked for all vital information. I had been assured that I would have it. I appeared to be receiving it. . . . Yet, in fact, the most vital information from the intercepted Japanese messages was withheld from me. This failure not only deprived me of essential facts. It misled me.

I was not supplied with any information of the intercepted messages showing that the Japanese government had divided Pearl Harbor into five areas and was seeking minute information as to the berthing of ships of the fleet in those areas, which was vitally significant.[160]

Admiral Kimmel testified under oath that "Had we been furnished this information as little as two or three hours before the attack, which was easily feasible and possible, much could have been done."[161]

At the time of the Pearl Harbor congressional hearings in 1945–1946, the only code the investigators knew that the Navy had broken was the diplomatic code. Much testimony was taken regarding what information was known in Washington by Roosevelt and Marshall concerning the diplomatic code and what was not passed along to Admiral Kimmel and General Short.[162] One of these important messages was that the Japanese indicated that if they were not able to secure a peace agreement with the Americans by November 26, 1941, things would automatically go into operation, indicating that an attack would occur after that point.

---

[160]Kimmel as quoted in Beach, *Scapegoats*, pp. 57–59.

[161]Morgenstern, *Pearl Harbor*, p. 253.

[162]The bomb-plot messages were not part of the diplomatic intercepts, but were messages from spies in Hawaii.

This was not delivered to the military commanders at Pearl Harbor.[163]

Another critical diplomatic code interception received in Washington and not delivered to Pearl Harbor was called the "winds execute" message, which was received during the night of December 3, 1941. Captain Laurence F. Safford received and translated the message to mean "War with America, War with England, and Peace with Russia."[164] The written evidence of the "winds execute" message mysteriously disappeared from Navy files before the first congressional investigation, but Captain Safford was absolutely certain of the receipt and content of the message and was certain that it was delivered to President Roosevelt immediately.[165]

Finally, the code interceptors received and translated a fourteen-part message from the Japanese government to its diplomats in Washington, D.C.; the first thirteen parts were received on December 6, 1941.[166] The first part of this message was delivered about 9:15 P.M. to Lieutenant Lester R. Schulz at the White House, and he immediately took the locked pouch containing the message to Roosevelt. Harry Hopkins, of course, was also present, and Schulz heard Roosevelt state to Hopkins, "This means war!" Hopkins then replied, "It's too bad we can't strike the first blow and prevent a surprise." Roosevelt replied, "No, we can't do that. We are a democracy and a peaceful people. But we have a good record!"[167]

There is a great deal of controversy about what transpired between this point and the actual bombing the next morning. However, Captain Edward L. Beach's recent book, *Scapegoats*, addresses the issue of why the fourteen-part message was not

---

[163]Ibid., p. 184.

[164]Bartlett, *Cover-Up*, p. 100; see also Morgenstern, *Pearl Harbor*, pp. 198–211.

[165]Ibid.

[166]Beach, *Scapegoats*, pp. 87–109.

[167]Ibid., p. 89.

delivered to the Pearl Harbor commanders. He references the new evidence concerning a meeting at midnight at the White House on December 6, which lasted until approximately 4:00 A.M. on December 7. According to Beach's book, James G. Stahlman, a close friend of Secretary of Navy Frank Knox, said that Knox told him he attended this meeting, along with Secretary of War Henry Stimson, General Marshall, Admiral Stark, Harry Hopkins, and Roosevelt. The purpose was to discuss the message already received and to review the fourteenth part of the message, which was expected to be delivered at any moment but did not come while the meeting was taking place. Stahlman did not report that Secretary Knox informed him about the actual content of the discussions, but one is led to surmise what occurred by the actions of the parties after their meeting during the early morning hours of December 7.[168] This particular decoded message has been called the "delivery message" which informed the Japanese diplomats that the fourteenth part of the message must be delivered to Secretary of State Hull on December 7 no later than 1:00 P.M. Washington time—which was dawn, Pearl Harbor time. The intent of the Japanese was to give notice to the American government that an attack was going to be made on Pearl Harbor just before the attack actually occurred, so that they could never be accused of launching a surprise attack. The fourteenth part was late in being delivered to Hull, but of course, the key people in Washington— especially Roosevelt and Marshall—had full knowledge of all the decoded messages before this, so the attack was clearly no "surprise" to them.

When Admiral Stark arrived at his office at 8:00 A.M. on December 7, he was met by Rear Admiral Theodore S. Wilkinson and Commander Arthur McCollum. These two officers had with them the first thirteen parts of the message and stated that they were waiting to receive the "delivery message," which arrived while they were meeting with Stark. Wilkinson indicated that it was absolutely imperative that Admiral Stark get on his scrambler telephone and issue a warning first to Admiral Kimmel in Pearl

---

[168]Ibid.; specifically for the letter of Stahlman, see pp. 203–05.

Harbor and then to Admiral Thomas C. Hart in Manila.[169] The scrambler telephone was an instrument that allowed direct and immediate contact between the parties, but the message was scrambled so it could not be intercepted and understood; however, at each end, it was unscrambled and immediately understood. Kimmel would have received this warning at 3:00 A.M. Pearl Harbor time, and that would have given him sufficient time to either prepare for or prevent the surprise attack. According to these witnesses, Stark picked up his scrambler telephone and hesitated for a long period of time, then put the phone down and instead tried to call President Roosevelt. The White House operator stated that the president was unavailable! The witnesses then stated that Stark tried to reach General Marshall, who was not in his office, and all witnesses agreed that Stark did nothing at all after that for the next few hours, until Marshall finally returned his call.[170]

The transcript of the Joint Congressional Committee hearings in 1945–1946 shows that General Marshall testified he had been riding his horse during the early morning hours of December 7, and that he did not arrive at his office until about 11:00 A.M. at which time he was given the complete, fourteen-part message by two of his most senior intelligence officers, Brigadier General Sherman Miles and Colonel Rufus Bratton. Marshall also had a scrambler telephone on his desk that would have allowed him to make a direct call to General Short, but instead of making the call he slowly and deliberately read through the message while both Miles and Bratton frantically tried to tell him about the crucial delivery message and the time limitation of 1:00 P.M. Washington time. Finally, with the office clock showing nearly noon, Marshall wrote out a warning message in pencil in nearly illegible handwriting and then told Miles and Bratton that the message was to be sent to Admiral Kimmel on a nonpriority basis. The message, therefore, went by normal Western Union telegram and arrived at Kimmel's

---

[169]Ibid., p. 95
[170]Ibid.

office after the attack had occurred.[171] General Marshall then returned the call to Admiral Stark, who had been waiting for about two hours to talk with him.

Admiral J.O. Richardson, the original commander at Pearl Harbor who was relieved by Roosevelt, wrote his memoirs in 1956 but delayed publication until 1973, a year after his friend Admiral Stark died and a year before Richardson's own death.[172] He gave his opinion that Stark and Marshall were under orders from President Roosevelt not to warn Kimmel and Short. Elsewhere Richardson has written:

> I am impelled to believe that sometime prior to December 7, the president had directed that only Marshall could send any warning message to the Hawaiian area. I do not know this to be a fact and I cannot prove it. I believe this because of my knowledge of Stark and the fact that his means of communications with Kimmel were equal to, if not superior to those available to Marshall for communication with Short. He made no effort to warn Kimmel on the morning of December 7, but referred the matter to Marshall.[173]

Captain Beach has also written:

> Richardson stated that he was positive that there had been "some directive from higher authority" that only Marshall was to make any such call, but he believed Stark should have done it anyway, and he never forgave him. Richardson was clearly outraged, and the entire Navy would have been also, had it known.[174]

The obvious question is, why would President Roosevelt not want Marshall and Stark to communicate the warnings to General Short and Admiral Kimmel at Pearl Harbor? During the Joint

---

[171]Ibid., pp. 96–97.

[172]Richardson, *On the Treadmill to Pearl Harbor.*

[173]Quoted by Beach, *Scapegoats*, p. 201.

[174]Ibid., p. 96.

Commission hearings, Senator Homer Ferguson of Michigan questioned General Short about what he thought would have happened had the commander at Pearl Harbor been notified of the impending attack. General Short testified:

> There would have been a very excellent chance that they would have turned back. . . . That would have been the tendency, because they would have felt, or they would be sure, that they would take heavy losses. Surprise was the only opportunity they had to succeed.[175]

The conclusion seems obvious: Roosevelt did not want to take a chance on the Japanese backing off from firing the first shot, and therefore he gambled that the losses would not be too heavy if the Japanese achieved total surprise. Unlike Lincoln at Fort Sumter, where no injuries or deaths occurred as a result of the South firing the first shot, Roosevelt suffered immense damages with his gamble.

Secretary of War Henry Stimson recorded in his diary the relief from the anxiety over the question of how to get into the war by the fact that the Japanese had now bombed Pearl Harbor. He wrote that at 2:00 P.M. on Sunday, December 7, he received a telephone call from the president informing him that the Japanese were bombing Pearl Harbor. He confided in his diary, "We three [Hull, Knox, and Stimson] all thought that we must fight if the British fought. *But now the Japs have solved the whole thing by attacking us directly in Hawaii.*"[176] Stimson also wrote in his diary:

> When the news first came that Japan had attacked us my first feeling was of relief that the indecision was over and that a crisis had come in a way which would unite all our people. This continued to be my dominant feeling in spite of the news of catastrophes which quickly developed. For I feel that this country united has practically nothing to fear; while the apathy and

---

[175]Morgenstern, *Pearl Harbor*, p. 259.
[176]Ibid., p. 308; emphasis in original.

divisions stirred up by unpatriotic men had been hitherto very discouraging.[177]

Morgenstern's editorial comment at this point about Stimson's diary entry is, "In other words, Stimson's view was that it was patriotic to go to war for the British and Dutch empires, and unpatriotic to try to stay at peace."[178] Stimson was clearly stating the viewpoint of the American portion of the Anglo-American Establishment which now was the combined Morgan and Rockefeller interests.[179] Murray Rothbard comments on the merger of the Morgan and Rockefeller efforts for the purpose of getting America into World War II:

> During the 1930s, the Rockefellers pushed hard for war against Japan, which they saw as competing with them vigorously for oil and rubber resources in Southeast Asia and as endangering the Rockefellers' cherished dreams of a mass "China market" for petroleum products. On the other hand, the Rockefellers took a non-interventionist position in Europe, where they had close financial ties with German firms such as I.G. Farben and Company, and very few close relations with Britain and France. The Morgans, in contrast, as usual deeply committed to their financial ties with Britain and France, once again plumped early for war with Germany, while their interest in the Far East had become minimal. Indeed, U.S. Ambassador to Japan, Joseph C. Grew, former Morgan partner, was one of the few officials in the Roosevelt Administration genuinely interested in peace with Japan.

---

[177]Ibid., p. 309.

[178]Ibid.

[179]Stimson was a close associate of the Morgan interests, a Wall Street lawyer and a protégé of Morgan's personal attorney, Elihu Root. He served as secretary of war for Presidents Taft and Franklin Roosevelt and as secretary of state under Herbert Hoover. See Rothbard, *Wall Street, Banks, and American Foreign Policy*, p. 18.

World War II might therefore be considered, from one point of view, as a coalition war: the Morgans got *their* war in Europe, the Rockefellers *theirs* in Asia.[180]

Roosevelt knew that if Japan entered the war, Germany would soon follow. One of the diplomatic messages intercepted by the Americans on November 29, 1941, was a conversation between the Japanese ambassador and Von Ribbentrop, the German foreign minister, in which Ribbentrop stated, "Should Japan become engaged in a war against the United States, Germany, of course, would join the war immediately."[181] On the night of December 7, 1941, after the bombing, Roosevelt summoned his cabinet members and congressional leaders to the White House to discuss the Pearl Harbor attack. He said to the assembled group that, "We have reason to believe that the Germans have told the Japanese that if Japan declares war, they will too. In other words, a declaration of war by Japan automatically brings . . ."[182] The president was interrupted at this point and did not finish his sentence, but this comment indicates clearly that he was familiar with the Japanese code intercepts and knew that an attack by Japan would open the back door to a war with Germany, and that was Roosevelt's real intention.

Roosevelt's defenders have maintained that adequate warnings were sent to the Pearl Harbor commanders by his administration in Washington. The following warnings were sent and are summarized by Morgenstern as follows[183];

1. On October 16, 1941, Kimmel received a message that a new cabinet had been formed in Japan and that war between Japan and Russia was a strong possibility. It was also stated that a possible war by Japan could occur with the U.S. and Britain.

---

[180]Ibid., pp. 27–28; emphasis in original.

[181]Morgenstern, *Pearl Harbor*, p. 189.

[182]Ibid., p. 298.

[183]Ibid., pp. 223–42.

2. On November 24, 1941, Admiral Kimmel received word that successful negotiations were doubtful and to look for a possible attack by Japan on the Philippines or Guam.

3. On November 25, 1941, there was a message which hardly constituted a warning at all.

4. On November 27, 1941, the message stated "consider this dispatch a war warning."[184] It speculated that the likely targets for Japan would be the Philippines, the Kar Peninsula or Borneo. The message specifically stated to take precautions against sabotage, which caused the airplanes to be moved to the middle portion of the airfield to guard against sabotage, but this made them an easy target to be bombed on December 7.

5. Finally, a second warning on November 27, 1941, stated that the negotiations with Japan had ended. This message included a specific statement that, "the United States desires that Japan commit first overt act." It also instructed Kimmel that they should not make any movements or demonstrate actions which might "alarm the civil population."[185]

It is obvious in comparing these warnings with all of the information that was known in Washington, but was not communicated to the Pearl Harbor commanders that Roosevelt did not want to destroy the surprise element and thereby take the chance that the Japanese would call off the attack and not fire the first shot. He needed to comply with his campaign promise that he would not go into a foreign war unless attacked first. He needed to comply with his commitment to Churchill and the British that he would get into the war against Germany by some means, even if it required going through the "back door" by having a war with Japan.

Cover-up

One of the first actions Roosevelt took after asking Congress for a declaration of war was to form a commission that was limited

---

184Ibid., p. 225.
185Ibid., p. 226.

in its scope to the investigation of what happened at Pearl Harbor to allow the surprise attack to succeed with such disastrous results. The directions to the committee specifically excluded any investigation of what went on in Washington, D.C.[186] This commission held secret hearings in Pearl Harbor; neither Commander Kimmel nor Short was allowed to submit any evidence or confront any witnesses, and they were completely denied due process. The commission concluded that these two commanding officers, Kimmel and Short, were solely at fault for the lack of preparation that caused the debacle. President Roosevelt had both of them reduced in rank and forced them to resign in disgrace.[187]

Stinnett reports the following reaction by the admiral who preceded Kimmel at Pearl Harbor: "Admiral James Richardson condemned the findings. 'It is the most unfair, unjust and deceptively dishonest document ever printed by the government printing office. I cannot conceive of honorable men serving on the commission without greatest regret and deepest feelings of shame.'"[188]

It was not until Stinnett's book was published that it was learned that the official cover-up began before the commission even began its work. Stinnett reports:

The key evidence of what really happened began to be concealed as early as December 11, 1941, only four days after the attack. The first step in the clean-up [cover-up] came from

---

[186]Ibid., p. 41; Roosevelt appointed Supreme Court Justice Owen J. Roberts as chairman of this commission. Justice Roberts had made a speech at Madison Square Garden on August 19, 1941, advocating America's entrance into the war as a means of achieving world government that he strongly supported.

[187]Ibid., pp. 38–50; and see Beach, *Scapegoats*, pp. 113–17. This is almost the same scenario that occurred with Captain Turner of the *Lusitania* in World War I, who was blamed for the disaster and made the scapegoat, thereby diverting the attention away from Churchill and the British government.

[188]Stinnett, *Day of Deceit*, p. 255.

Rear Admiral Leigh Noyes, the Navy's Director of Communications. He instituted the fifty-four-year censorship policy that consigned the pre-Pearl Harbor Japanese military and diplomatic intercepts and the relevant directives to Navy vaults. "Destroy all notes or anything in writing," Noyes told a group of his subordinates on December 11.[189]

Stinnett shows how the cover-up continued even after the war:

> Two weeks after Japan surrendered in August 1945, the Navy blocked public access to the pre-Pearl Harbor intercepts by classifying the documents TOP SECRET. Even Congress was cut out of the intercept loop. The Navy's order was sweeping; it gagged the cryptographers and radio intercept operators who had obtained the Japanese fleet's radio messages during the fall of 1941. Fleet Admiral Ernest King oversaw the censorship. He threatened imprisonment and loss of Navy and veteran's benefits to any naval personnel who disclosed the success of the code-breaking.
>
> When the congressional investigation into the Pearl Harbor attack began on November 15, 1945, Americans believed they would be given full details on breaking the Japanese code prior to the attack. Witnesses introduced intercepts into evidence and read decrypted messages to the senators and representatives of the Joint Committee. It was a total sham. None of the details involving the interception, decoding, or dissemination of the pre-Pearl Harbor Japanese naval messages saw the light of day. Only diplomatic messages were released. Republicans suspected a stranglehold but could not pierce King's gag order.[190]

It was not until May 1999, almost fifty-eight years later, that the U.S. Senate held another hearing and tried to rectify this grave injustice inflicted by President Roosevelt upon these capable career officers by making them the scapegoats for the "surprise attack" on Pearl Harbor. A Senate resolution posthumously

---

[189]Ibid.

[190]Ibid., pp. 256–57.

restored their full rank and declared that both men had performed their duties "completely and professionally" and that the Japanese attack was "not a result of dereliction of the performance" of their duties.[191] The U.S. Senate further made an extremely important finding:

> Numerous investigations following the attack on Pearl Harbor have documented that then Admiral Kimmel and then Lieutenant General Short were not provided necessary and critical intelligence that was available, that foretold of war with Japan, that warned of imminent attack, and that would have alerted them to prepare for the attack, including such essential communiques as the Japanese Pearl Harbor Bomb Plot message of September 24, 1941, and the message sent from the Imperial Japanese Foreign Ministry to the Japanese Ambassador in the United States from December 6–7, 1941, known as the Fourteen-Part Message.[192]

The Senate did not know about the sensational revelations in Robert Stinnett's book, which was published after the hearings. Perhaps someday the American people will finally understand that the real reason the day of December 7, 1941, will "live in infamy" will be because their president had become an "imperial president" who betrayed the American servicemen at Pearl Harbor and badly misled the U.S. Congress and the American people into an unnecessary war.

Stinnett's book reveals the ugly truth of the crimes, if not treason, of President Roosevelt and leaves no doubt about how Roosevelt provoked the Japanese into firing the first shot and how he withheld essential information from his Pearl Harbor commanders that would have allowed them either to prevent the attack or protect themselves. The book further shows the massive

---

[191]See Roth Amendment No. 388 to the Defense Authorization Act passed by the United States Senate for the 106th Congress, First Session May 25, 1999, and the Senate Congressional Record for May 24, 1999, Sec. 582, p. S 5879.

[192]Ibid., Senate Congressional Record, p. 5878.

cover-up instigated by President Roosevelt. It further shows the sinister conspiracy instigated by the president and carried out by his military and civilian subordinates to make Admiral Kimmel and General Short the scapegoats by diverting the attention away from the political intrigue in Washington. The book confirms that the power of the presidency and the executive branch has led to deceit and corruption similar to the worst Caesars of Rome. The Roosevelt supporters are now reduced to the erroneous, ridiculous, and evil Machiavellian defense that the end (war with Germany) justified the means (provoking the Japanese to fire the first shot by sacrificing the men and ships at Pearl Harbor).

5

LINCOLN AND ROOSEVELT: AMERICAN CAESARS

IT IS INTERESTING TO compare Lincoln and his treachery in causing the Southern "enemy" to fire the first shot at Fort Sumter, resulting in the Civil War, with Roosevelt's similar manipulation causing the attack on Pearl Harbor and America's entry into World War II.

Arthur M. Schlesinger, Jr., a well-known American "court historian," has written the definitive defenses for both Abraham Lincoln and Franklin D. Roosevelt regarding their reprehensible behavior in causing their respective unnecessary American wars. He clearly documents the unconstitutional behavior of both and offers great praise for the same. He attempts to justify the actions of both presidents on grounds that they were acting during a "crisis" pertaining to the "survival of the American government," and that their unconstitutional actions were thereby made "necessary." Schlesinger has stated that "Next to the Civil War, World War II was the greatest crisis in American history."[1] His defense of these two "great" presidents is as follows:

> Roosevelt in 1941, like Lincoln in 1861, did what he did under what appeared to be a *popular demand* and a *public necessity*.

---

[1]Arthur M. Schlesinger, Jr., *The Imperial Presidency* (Boston: Houghton Mifflin, 1973), p. 116.

Both presidents took their actions in light of day and to the accompaniment of *uninhibited political debate*. They did what they thought they had to do to *save the republic*. They threw themselves in the end on the justice of the country and the rectitude of their motives. Whatever Lincoln and Roosevelt felt compelled to do under the pressure of crisis did not corrupt their essential commitment to constitutional ways and democratic processes.[2]

Schlesinger, however, recognizes the terrible precedents that were created by these presidents' violations of the clear Constitutional restrictions on their office:

> Yet the danger persists that power asserted during *authentic emergencies* may create precedents for transcendent executive power during emergencies that exist only in the hallucinations of the Oval Office and that remain invisible to most of the nation. The perennial question is: How to distinguish real crises threatening the life of the republic from bad dreams conjured up by paranoid presidents spurred on by paranoid advisers? Necessity as Milton said, is always "the tyrant's plea."[3]

Let us add to John Milton's statement a more specific warning by William Pitt in his speech to the House of Commons on November 18, 1783: "Necessity is the plea for every infringement of human freedom. It is the argument of tyrants."[4]

Finally, it is instructive to compare the circumstances for Lincoln at Fort Sumter with those for Roosevelt at Pearl Harbor. In neither case was there an actual "surprise" attack by the enemy.

---

[2]Arthur M. Schlesinger, Jr., "War and the Constitution: Abraham Lincoln and Franklin D. Roosevelt," in *Lincoln, the War President: The Gettysburg Lectures*, Gabor S. Boritt, ed. (New York: Oxford University Press, 1992), p. 174; emphasis added.

[3]Ibid., p. 176; emphasis added.

[4]John Bartlett, *Familiar Quotations*, Emily Morrison Beck, ed., 14th ed. (Boston: Little, Brown, 1968), p. 496.

In fact, there was an extended period of time, many months prior to the "first shot," in which both Lincoln and Roosevelt had ample opportunity to attempt to negotiate with the alleged "enemy," who was desperately trying to reach a peaceful settlement. In both cases, the presidents refused to negotiate in good faith. Lincoln sent completely false and conflicting statements to the Confederates and to Congress; even refused to talk with the Confederate commissioners. Roosevelt also refused to talk with Japanese Prime Minister Konoye, a refusal that brought down the moderate, peace-seeking Konoye government and caused the rise of the militant Tojo regime. Both Lincoln and Roosevelt repeatedly lied to the American people and to Congress about what they were doing while they were secretly provoking the "enemy" to fire the first shot in their respective wars. Both intentionally subjected their respective armed forces to being bait to get the enemy to fire the first shot.

Also, a comparison of circumstances clearly shows that both Lincoln and Roosevelt had ample opportunity to present their arguments and the question of war to Congress as the Constitution clearly required them to do. In fact, Congress in both cases was desperately trying to find out what the presidents were doing, and in both cases the presidents were hiding evidence from them. In Lincoln's case, Congress probably would not have declared war for either the real reasons Lincoln went to war or for those he used only for propaganda. Similarly, Roosevelt could have presented the question of war to Congress and attempted to persuade Congress and the American people that we needed to join Soviet Russia and Great Britain to fight tyranny in Germany. This might have been embarrassing to the Roosevelt administration in light of the fact that Congress may not have wanted to declare war and join with Soviet Russia, which was already one of the greatest tyrannies the world had ever known, while Germany was Russia's main enemy. A majority in Congress surely were aware of the dangers of Communism, while Roosevelt never seemed to grasp the total evil of Stalin or Communism. Roosevelt gave Stalin everything he wanted throughout the war and referred to this mass murderer as "Uncle Joe." The wartime conferences at Teheran and Yalta clearly demonstrated Roosevelt's complete and secret capitulation to Communism in Russia and China.[5]

Before World War II started in Europe in 1939, it was widely known that Stalin had already murdered more than ten million innocent, unarmed people, three million of whom were Russian peasants he killed between 1928 and 1935. Communism believed that private property was the main source of evil in the world, and therefore he took the privately owned land from these self-sufficient people.[6] Also, in the period from 1936 through 1938, Stalin murdered millions more during his reign of terror after the "show trials," purging from the Communist Party those he thought were disloyal.[7] Hitler, on the other hand, before 1939, and primarily from June to July 1934, had murdered fewer than one hundred in his purge of the Storm Troopers.[8] This is not to defend Hitler, or to deny that he was evil, but a comparison of these two murderers and tyrants (as Stalin and Hitler were known in the period from 1939 to 1941), shows that Roosevelt could hardly have asked Congress to declare war and to join with Stalin and Communism, yet still argue that he was fighting a noble war against tyranny.

Private Enterprise Compared with Free Enterprise

Another interesting comparison of the situations affecting the decisions of Lincoln and Roosevelt is that economic interests of an elite few played a major role in the decisions of both presidents

---

[5]George N. Crocker, *Roosevelt's Road to Russia* (Chicago: Henry Regnery, 1959); and for an explanation of Roosevelt's delivery of China to the communists, see Anthony Kubek, *How the Far East Was Lost: American Policy and the Creation of Communist China, 1941–1949* (Chicago: Henry Regnery, 1963); see also Perlmutter, *FDR and Stalin*.

[6]R.J. Rummel, *Death by Government* (New Brunswick, N.J.: Transaction Publishers, 1995), p. 10; see also Robert Conquest, *The Harvest of Sorrow: Soviet Collectivization and the Terror-Famine* (New York: Oxford University Press, 1986).

[7]Rummel, *Death by Government*, p. 10; see generally Robert Conquest, *The Great Terror: Stalin's Purge of the Thirties* (New York: Macmillan, 1968).

[8]Rummel, *Death by Government*, pp. 111–22.

to instigate a war. It is doubtful that either Lincoln or Roosevelt would have wanted to disclose the influence of these economic interests to the public in a congressional hearing where the question of war was to be decided upon. The study of the history of wars indicates that economic factors have always played a major role in starting wars, but rarely are these economic factors disclosed to the public as the reasons.

Many businessmen and bankers believe in *private* enterprise but do not believe in *free* enterprise. In Lincoln's case, the private-enterprise capitalists wanted Lincoln to have a war in order to prevent the South from establishing a free-trade zone with a low tariff. They wanted Lincoln to protect their special interests by keeping the tariff high, while still forcing the South to remain in the Union to pay the tax. These types of people want a partnership between private enterprise and the government, which is the essence of fascism and the cause of many wars. In the case of Roosevelt, he was greatly influenced, even controlled at times, by the Anglo-American Establishment that was composed of prominent businessmen and bankers who owned or represented large economic interests, both domestically and globally. They also wanted a partnership with government to protect their private businesses and economic interests, especially from formidable industrial and commercial competitors like Germany and Japan. Today the economic establishment in America is much larger than just the Morgan and Rockefeller interests but is just as active in trying to influence government, especially the foreign policy; primarily through the president to further their economic interests.

Ludwig von Mises made a clear distinction between private enterprise and free enterprise. Mises wanted a complete separation of the economy from the government, just like separation of church and state, which meant no regulation or control by the government but also no partnership with or help from the government, either economically or militarily. In the free-enterprise system, if any business or any bank wants to transact business globally, it must do so at its own risk and without the help of the government. There would be no foreign aid, especially no aid to prop up dictators in order for them to do business with any particular economic interests. There would be no war in order to create a devastated area like Bosnia or Yugoslavia that needs to be rebuilt by American businesses who have the political influence to get these foreign contracts. Mises thought that separation of the economy from the government was necessary in order to produce peace rather than war.

A major contribution of Mises and the Austrian School of economics is to show that government intervention and regulation of the economy is the actual cause of the boom and bust cycles, while a free market is very stable and self-correcting in a short period of time. Furthermore, Mises showed that coercive monopolies are created by government and not by the free market. Therefore, the economy does not need government regulation or control to stabilize it and will function better by being completely separated.

Mises's other recommendation, seen in the following statement, is to reduce the size and power of the central government in general in order to protect individual liberty:

> Durable peace is only possible under *perfect capitalism*, hitherto never and nowhere completely tried or achieved. In such a Jeffersonian world of unhampered market economy the scope of government activities is limited to the protection of the lives, health and property of individuals against violence or fraudulent aggression.[9]

Mises goes on to state that:

> All the oratory of the advocates of government omnipotence cannot annul the fact that there is but one system that makes for durable peace: a free market economy. Government control leads to economic nationalism and thus results in conflict.[10]

---

[9]Ludwig von Mises, *Omnipotent Government: The Rise of the Total State and Total War* (New Rochelle, N.Y.: Arlington House, 1969), p. 284; emphasis added.

[10]Ibid., p. 286.

This complete separation of the economy and the government is what Mises meant by "perfect capitalism," which promotes peace and prosperity rather than war and welfare.

Foreign Influence—The Anglo-American Establishment

In Roosevelt's case, a foreign government clearly influenced and literally worked secretly and directly with him to cause the U.S. to enter World War II in complete violation of President Washington's warning in his *Farewell Address* against allowing the influence of foreign governments to control American policy. This is still a major problem today with America's foreign policy. American political leaders have not only ignored President Washington's warning about the dangerous influence of foreign powers, but they have also ignored his excellent advice that we should avoid permanent entangling alliances, such as the United Nations and NATO. Washington advised us to have as little *political* connection with other governments as possible, while having *trade* relationships with *all* and without preferential status. Mises and President Washington are not advocating isolationism; they are advocating global trade with all nations.

President Washington warned emphatically against getting involved in the quarrels of Europe. Under President Clinton, the U.S. readopted the Wilsonian foreign policy of crusading throughout the world as its policeman by disguising imperialism with the term "humanitarianism," a policy that involves American armed forces in matters which have no relationship to real American interests or the defense of the American people and their homeland. Many members of Congress are now calling for the draft again in order to have enough soldiers to be the world's policeman. Charles Beard, the famous historian, warned that we would lose our freedom if we adopted a policy of "perpetual war for perpetual peace,"[11] and it was one of our Founders, James Madison, who warned that, "No nation could preserve its freedom in the midst of continual warfare."[12] War necessarily concentrates political power

---

[11]Harry Elmer Barnes, ed., *Perpetual War for Perpetual Peace*, p. viii.

[12]James Madison, "Political Observations," *Letters and Other Writings of James Madison (1795)* (Philadelphia: J.B. Lippincott, 1865), vol. 4, pp.

into the hands of a few—especially the president—and diminishes the liberty of all.

Reclaiming the Dream of Our Founders

If Americans are to reclaim the dream of our Founders and have peace and prosperity instead of war and welfare, we must understand the ideas and institutions that promote those conditions. Americans must appreciate and adopt the free-enterprise system and reject the private-enterprise system. Since the beginning of the twentieth century, we have been on a collision course with disaster by following political leaders who got elected and maintained their power through the war and welfare system of politics. Americans will never reclaim the dream of their Founders if presidents like Lincoln and Roosevelt are held up as examples of "great" presidents. We must impeach those presidents who ignore that the Constitution grants the war-making power exclusively to Congress, and certainly impeach those who mislead Congress into a declaration of war with false information.

Americans need to oppose and destroy the "imperial presidency" because of what it has already done and will do to our country and to our individual freedom. The first step toward that goal is to recognize Presidents Lincoln and Roosevelt for what they really were: American Caesars.

491–92; also see further quotations from Madison in John V. Denson, "War and American Freedom," in *The Costs of War: America's Pyrrhic Victories*, John V. Denson, ed. (New Brunswick, N.J.: Transaction Publishers, 1999), pp. 6–11.

$$6$$

ANOTHER CENTURY OF WAR?

MOST LIBERTARIANS, OR BELIEVERS in the free market economy, probably met professor Gabriel Kolko through reading his 1963 revisionist interpretation of American economic history for the period of 1900 to 1916, entitled *The Triumph of Conservatism*. Since then, professor Kolko has been primarily a historian of war and American foreign policy which culminated in his 1994 *magnum opus* entitled *Century of War: Politics, Conflicts and Society Since 1914*. The publisher of this work suggested that he continue the same theme by commenting upon the events of September 11, 2001. The result is this excellent one-hundred-fifty-page book published in 2002, *Another Century of War?*, written in a very readable, journalistic style. Kolko states the purpose of his book:

> In the following pages I outline some of the causes for the events of September 11 and why America's foreign policies not only have failed to exploit communism's demise but have become both more destabilizing and counterproductive. I also try to answer the crucial question posed in my title: Will there be another century of war?

Professor Kolko's theme is that the United States has become the single most important arms exporter, thereby contributing to much of the disorder in the world, and furthermore, contrary to America's claims of bringing stability to the world by its interventions, especially since 1947 in the Middle East, it has caused death, destruction and turmoil. America has become the sole rogue superpower and is no longer restrained by the possibility of the Soviet Union throwing a counterpunch. Kolko states:

> Communism virtually ceased to exist over a decade ago, depriving the United States of the primary justification for its foreign and military policies since 1945.

Kolko points out that America struggled to find an appropriate major enemy but finally targeted China, which was trying to discard its communism and establish a free market economy. However, September 11 changed everything. Terrorism has become the worldwide enemy of America which may result in a perpetual war to oppose this sinister and elusive enemy. He points out further that: "Bush had campaigned in 2000 as a critic of 'big government,' but after September 11 he became an 'imperial' president with new, draconian powers over civil liberties."

In regard to our policies in the Middle East since 1948, he says we tried to keep Soviet Russia out and take over more control of British oil interests, while assuming their contradictory policy of supporting the state of Israel and remaining friendly to the surrounding Arab states. Kolko shows that we supported the Shah in Iran while the CIA and the Israeli Mossad trained the Shah's secret police, the SAVAK. The Shah was overthrown, largely as a result of the revolt against the oppression by his secret police. We then armed and supported Saddam Hussein in Iraq, giving him a massive amount of weapons, and along with Saudi Arabia, much money, in order to fight the new leaders of Iran.

Furthermore, he states that the CIA set up a Vietnam-type trap for the Soviet Union in Afghanistan, and with financial assistance from Saudi Arabia, we armed and supplied Osama bin Ladin in order to fight the Soviets. When Saddam and Iraq threatened Kuwait, Osama bin Ladin offered to repel Saddam but this offer was refused. Instead, the American coalition, with financial support from Saudi Arabia, pushed Saddam back within his borders while leaving American troops in Saudi Arabia, thus alienating bin Ladin, who vowed vengeance on America for this act. Bin Ladin mobilized his forces into the al-Qaeda in 1989, by training up to 70,000 potential fighters and terrorists while creating cells in at least 50 countries, all initially financed with U.S. and Saudi money. Kolko states: "But both of America's prime enemies in the Islamic world today—Osama bin Ladin and Saddam Hussein in Iraq—were for much of the 1980s its close allies and friends, whom it sustained and encouraged with arms and much else."

Kolko points out that American wars and various interventions have usually produced unintended consequences which were harmful to the best interests of America. He concludes his critique of American foreign policy in the Middle East with the following statement:

> All of its [America's] policies in the Middle East have been contradictory and counterproductive. The United States' support for Israel is the most important but scarcely the only cause of the September 11 trauma and the potentially fundamental political destabilization, ranging from the Persian Gulf to South Asia, that its intervention in Afghanistan has triggered.

Kolko states that our massive support for Israel, which began in 1968, was one of the turning points in American foreign policy:

> This aid [to Israel] reached $600 million in 1971 (seven times the amount under the entire Johnson administration) and over $2 billion in 1973. Thenceforth, Israel became the leading recipient of U.S. arms aid. Today it still receives about $3 billion in free American aid. Most of the Arab world, quite understandably, has since identified Israel and the United States as one.

He points out further that our invasion of Afghanistan has greatly destabilized the governments of Pakistan and Saudi Arabia, which may produce even worse results for America.

American foreign policy will now try to justify its huge military budgets to fight terrorism, but terrorism is the guerrilla warfare weapon of the weak against the strong, and is not overcome with huge defense budgets, large armies and navies or high-tech airplanes. He quotes Secretary of Defense Donald Rumsfeld, however, who maintains that:

> We are perfectly capable of spending whatever we need to spend. The world economy depends on the United States [contributing] to peace and stability. That is what underpins the economic health of the world, including the United States.

Professor Kolko paints a dire future for America if it continues its frequent interventions and warfare throughout the world:

> Should it confront the forty or more nations that now have terrorist networks, then it will in one manner or another intervene everywhere. . . . America has power without wisdom, and cannot recognize the limits of arms despite its repeated experiences. The result has been folly, and hatred, which is a recipe for disasters. September 11 confirmed that. The war has come home.

Kolko summarizes American foreign policy and its results as follows:

> The United States after 1947 attempted to guide and control a very large part of the change that occurred throughout the world, and a significant part of what is wrong with it today is the result of America's interventions.

He states that we do not have to look at political arguments or even Washington's Farewell Address to see what our policy should be in the future:

> The strongest argument against one nation interfering with another does not have to be deduced from any doctrine, moral or otherwise; it is found by looking honestly at the history of the past centuries.

He concludes with the sweeping statement that:

> Since the beginning of the last century, only wars have tested to their very foundations the stability of existing social systems, and communism, fascism, and Nazism would certainly not have triumphed without the events of 1914–18 to foster them.

Kolko concludes his final chapter by stating that we cannot afford further interventions and wars since weapons of mass destruction are prevalent throughout the world and available to terrorists everywhere:

> A foreign policy that is both immoral and unsuccessful is not simply stupid, it is increasingly dangerous to those who practice or favor it. That is the predicament that the United States now confronts.

He further states:

> The way America's leaders are running the nation's foreign policy is not creating peace or security at home or stability abroad. The reverse is the case: its interventions have been counterproductive. Everyone—Americans and those people who are objects of their efforts—would be far better off if the United States did nothing, closed its bases overseas and withdrew its fleets everywhere, and allowed the rest of the world to find its own way without American weapons and troops.

This little book is so full of wisdom and good common sense, that it should lead the way towards reaffirming our original foreign policy of noninterventionism, so well stated by Presidents Washington and Jefferson. American foreign policy changed to interventionism with the Spanish-American War, and all of its subsequent wars have actually diminished the freedom of the American people and caused death and destruction throughout the world. The difference now is that terrorism from the Arab world will be prevalent on our own shores rather than in a distant Europe or Asia, as in past wars. Kolko has written a powerful warning to the politicians of the "American Empire" about the danger of hubris, or the arrogance of power, showing that we should abandon our interventionist foreign policy or suffer the same consequences as other empires (e.g., Athenian, Roman, Spanish and British) before us. After all, our founders clearly warned us that we would retain our freedom only so long as we remained a Republic with limited powers in the central government and followed a noninterventionist foreign policy.

7

THE WILL TO PEACE

THE CHRISTMAS TRUCE, WHICH occurred primarily between the British and German soldiers along the Western Front in December 1914, is an event the official histories of the "Great War" leave out, and the Orwellian historians hide from the public. Stanley Weintraub has broken through this barrier of silence and written a moving account of this significant event by compiling letters sent home from the front, as well as diaries of the soldiers involved. His book is entitled *Silent Night: The Story of the World War I Christmas Truce*. The book contains many pictures of the actual events showing the opposing forces mixing and celebrating together that first Christmas of the war. This remarkable story begins to unfold, according to Weintraub, on the morning of December 19, 1914:

> Lieutenant Geoffrey Heinekey, new to the 2nd Queen's West-minister Rifles, wrote to his mother, "A most extraordinary thing happened. . . . Some Germans came out and held up their hands and began to take in some of their wounded and so we ourselves immediately got out of our trenches and began bringing in our wounded also. The Germans then beckoned to us and a lot of us went over and talked to them and they helped us to bury our dead. This lasted the whole morning and I talked to several of them and I must say they seemed extraordinarily fine men. . . . It seemed too ironical for words. There, the night before we had been having a terrific battle and the morning after, there we were smoking their cigarettes and they smoking ours."

Weintraub reports that the French and Belgians reacted differently to the war and with more emotion than the British in the beginning. The war was occurring on their land and "The French had lived in an atmosphere of *revanche* since 1870, when Alsace and Lorraine were seized by the Prussians" in a war declared by the French. The British and German soldiers, however, saw little meaning in the war as to them, and, after all, the British King and the German Kaiser were both grandsons of Queen Victoria. Why should the Germans and British be at war, or hating each other, because a royal couple from Austria were killed by an assassin while they were visiting in Bosnia? However, since August when the war started, hundreds of thousands of soldiers had been killed, wounded or missing by December 1914.

It is estimated that over eighty thousand young Germans had gone to England before the war to be employed in such jobs as waiters, cooks, and cab drivers and many spoke English very well. It appears that the Germans were the instigators of this move towards a truce. So much interchange had occurred across the lines by the time that Christmas Eve approached that Brigadier General G.T. Forrestier-Walker issued a directive forbidding fraternization:

> For it discourages initiative in commanders, and destroys offensive spirit in all ranks. . . . Friendly intercourse with the enemy, unofficial armistices and exchange of tobacco and other comforts, however tempting and occasionally amusing they may be, are absolutely prohibited.

Later strict orders were issued that any fraternization would result in a court-martial. Most of the seasoned German soldiers had been sent to the Russian front while the youthful and somewhat untrained Germans, who were recruited first, or quickly volunteered, were sent to the Western Front at the beginning of the war. Likewise, in England young men rushed to join in the war for the personal glory they thought they might achieve and many were afraid the war might end before they could get to the front. They had no idea this war would become one of attrition and conscription or that it would set the trend for the whole twentieth century, the bloodiest in history which became known as the War and Welfare Century.

As night fell on Christmas Eve the British soldiers noticed the Germans putting up small Christmas trees along with candles at the top of their trenches and many began to shout in English "We no shoot if you no shoot." The firing stopped along the many miles of the trenches and the British began to notice that the Germans were coming out of the trenches toward the British who responded by coming out to meet them. They mixed and mingled in No Man's Land and soon began to exchange chocolates for cigars and various newspaper accounts of the war which contained the propaganda from their respective homelands. Many of the officers on each side attempted to prevent the event from occurring but the soldiers ignored the risk of a court-martial or of being shot.

Some of the meetings reported in diaries were between Anglo-Saxons and German Saxons and the Germans joked that they should join together and fight the Prussians. The massive amount of fraternization, or maybe just the Christmas spirit, deterred the officers from taking action and many of them began to go out into No Man's Land and exchange Christmas greetings with their opposing officers. Each side helped bury their dead and remove the wounded so that by Christmas morning there was a large open area about as wide as the size of two football fields separating the opposing trenches. The soldiers emerged again on Christmas morning and began singing Christmas carols, especially *Silent Night*. They recited the 23rd Psalm together and played soccer and football. Again, Christmas gifts were exchanged and meals were prepared openly and attended by the opposing forces. Weintraub quotes one soldier's observation of the event: "Never . . . was I so keenly aware of the insanity of war."

The first official British history of the war came out in 1926 which indicated that the Christmas Truce was a very insignificant matter with only a few people involved. However, Weintraub states:

"During a House of Commons debate on March 31, 1930, Sir H. Kinglsey Wood, a Cabinet Minister during the next war, and a Major "In the front trenches" at Christmas 1914, recalled that he "took part in what was well known at the time as a truce. We went over in front of the trenches and shook hands with many of our German enemies. A great number of people [now] think we did something that was degrading." Refusing to presume that, he went on, "The fact is that we did it, and I then came to the conclusion that I have held very firmly ever since, that if we had been left to ourselves there would never have been another shot fired. For a fortnight the truce went on. We were on the most friendly terms, and it was only the fact that we were being controlled by others that made it necessary for us to start trying to shoot one another again." He blamed the resumption of the war on "the grip of the political system which was bad, and I and others who were there at the time determined there and then never to rest. . . . Until we had seen whether we could change it." But they could not.

Beginning with the French Revolution, one of the main ideas coming out of the nineteenth century, which became dominant at the beginning of the twentieth century, was nationalism with unrestrained democracy. In contrast, the ideas which led to the American Revolution were those of a federation of sovereign states joined together under the Constitution which severely limited and separated the powers of the national or central government in order to protect individual liberty. National democracy was restrained by a Bill of Rights. These ideas came into direct conflict with the beginning of the American War Between the States out of which nationalism emerged victorious. A principal idea of nationalism was that the individual owed a duty of self-sacrifice to "The Greater Good" of his nation and that the noblest act a person could do was to give his life for his country during a war, which would, in turn, bring him immortal fame.

Two soldiers, one British and one German, both experienced the horrors of the trench warfare in the Great War and both wrote moving accounts which challenged the idea of the glory of a sacrifice of the individual to the nation in an unnecessary or unjust war. The British soldier, Wilfred Owen, wrote a famous poem before he was killed in the trenches seven days before the Armistice was signed on November 11, 1918. He tells of the horror of the gas warfare which killed many in the trenches and ends with the following lines:

If in some smothering dreams you too could pace
Behind the wagon that we flung him in,
And watch the white eyes writhing in his face,
His hanging face, like a devil's sick of sin;
If you could hear, at every jolt, the blood
Come gargling from the froth-corrupted lungs,
Obscene as cancer, bitter as the cud
Of vile, incurable sores on innocent tongues—
My friend, you would not tell with such high zest
To children ardent for some desperate glory
The old Lie: Dulce et decorum est
Pro patria mori.[1]

The German soldier was Erich M. Remarque who wrote one of the best anti-war novels of all time, entitled *All Quiet On The Western Front*, which was later made into an American movie that won the 1930 Academy Award for Best Picture. He also attacked the idea of the nobility of dying for your country in an unnecessary war and he describes the suffering in the trenches:

We see men living with their skulls blown open; We see soldiers run with their two feet cut off; They stagger on their splintered stumps into the next shell-hole; A lance corporal crawls a mile and half on his hands dragging his smashed knee after him; Another goes to the dressing station and over his clasped hands bulge his intestines; We see men without mouths, without jaws, without faces; We find one man who has held the artery of his arm in his teeth for two hours in order not to bleed to death.

Thomas Hardy's poem "The Man He Killed," was published in 1902 and was inspired by the Boer War but it captures the spirit of the Christmas Truce in 1914:

---

[1]The Latin phrase is translated roughly as "It is sweet and honorable to die for one's country," a line from the Roman poet Horace used to produce patriotic zeal for ancient Roman wars.

Had he and I but met
By some old ancient inn,
We should have sat us down to wet
Right many a nipperkin!
But ranged as infantry,
And staring face to face,
I shot at him as he at me,
And killed him in his place.
I shot him dead because—
Because he was my foe,
Just so: my foe of course he was;
That's clear enough; although
He thought he'd 'list, perhaps,
Off-hand like—just as I—
Was out of work — had sold his traps—
No other reason why.
Yes, quaint and curious war is!
You shoot a fellow down
You'd treat if met where any bar is,
Or help to half-a-crown.

The last chapter of Weintraub's book is entitled "What If— ?" This is counterfactual history at its best and he sets out what he believes the rest of the twentieth century would have been like if the soldiers had been able to cause the Christmas Truce of 1914 to stop the war at that point. Like many other historians, he believes that with an early end of the war in December of 1914, there probably would have been no Russian Revolution, no Communism, no Lenin, and no Stalin. Furthermore, there would have been no vicious peace imposed on Germany by the Versailles Treaty, and therefore, no Hitler, no Nazism and no World War II. With the early truce there would have been no entry of America into the European War and America might have had a chance to remain, or return, to being a Republic rather than moving toward World War II, the "Cold" War (Korea and Vietnam), and our present status as the world bully.

Weintraub states that:

Franklin D. Roosevelt, only an obscure assistant secretary of the navy—of a fleet going nowhere militarily—would have returned to a boring law practice, and never have been the losing but attractive vice presidential candidate in 1920, a role earned by his war visibility. Wilson, who would not be campaigning for reelection in 1916 on a platform that he kept America out of war, would have lost (he only won narrowly) to a powerful new Republican president, Charles Evans Hughes.

He also suggests another result of the early peace:

Germany in peace rather than war would have become the dominant nation in Europe, possibly in the world, competitor to a more slowly awakening America, and to an increasingly ambitious and militant Japan. No Wilsonian League of Nations would have emerged. . . . Yet, a relatively benign, German-led, Commonwealth of Europe might have developed decades earlier than the European Community under leaders not destroyed in the war or its aftermath.

Many leaders of the British Empire saw the new nationalistic Germany (since 1870–1871) as a threat to their world trade, especially with Germany's new navy. The idea that economics played a major role in bringing on the war was confirmed by President Woodrow Wilson after the war in a speech wherein he gave his assessment of the real cause of the war. He was campaigning in St. Louis, Missouri in September of 1919 trying to get the U.S. Senate to approve the Versailles Treaty and he stated:

Why, my fellow-citizens, is there any man here, or any woman—let me say, is there any child here, who does not know that the seed of war in the modern world is industrial and commercial rivalry? . . . This war, in its inception, was a commercial and industrial war. It was not a political war.[2]

Weintraub alludes to a play by William Douglas Home entitled *A Christmas Truce* wherein characters representing British and German soldiers have just finished a soccer game in No Man's

---

[2]*The Papers of Woodrow Wilson*, Arthur S. Link, ed. (Princeton, N.J.: Princeton University Press, 1990), vol. 63, pp. 45–46.

Land on Christmas day and are engaged in a conversation which very well could represent the feelings of the soldiers on that day. The German lieutenant concedes the impossibility of the war ending as the soccer game had just done, with no bad consequences—"Because the Kaiser and the generals and the politicians in my country order us that we fight."

"So do ours," agrees Andrew Wilson (the British soldier).

"Then what can we do?"

"The answer's 'nothing.' But if we do nothing . . . like we're doing now, and go on doing it, there'll be nothing they can do but send us home."

"Or shoot us."

The Great War killed over ten million soldiers and Weintraub states, "Following the final Armistice came an imposed peace in 1919 that created new instabilities ensuring another war." This next war killed more than fifty million people, over half of whom were civilians. Weintruab writes:

> To many, the end of the war and the failure of the peace would validate the Christmas cease-fire as the only meaningful episode in the apocalypse. It belied the bellicose slogans and suggested that the men fighting and often dying were, as usual, proxies for governments and issues that had little to do with their everyday lives. A candle lit in the darkness of Flanders, the truce flickered briefly and survives only in memoirs, letters, song, drama and story.

Weintraub concludes his remarkable book with the following:

> A celebration of the human spirit, the Christmas Truce remains a moving manifestation of the absurdities of war. A very minor Scottish poet of Great War vintage, Frederick Niven, may have got it right in his "A Carol from Flanders," which closed,

> *O ye who read this truthful rime From Flanders, kneel and say:*
> *God speed the time when every day*
> *Shall be as Christmas Day.*

APPENDIX

ROOSEVELT, PEARL HARBOR, AND THE RED CROSS

ANOTHER REVELATION OF THE treachery of Roosevelt has been disclosed in *The Washington Times* section entitled "Inside the Beltway" for the April 22, 1999 issue. This newspaper report refers to an article by Daryl S. Borgquist, a Justice Department media affairs officer. The article, "Advance Warning: The Red Cross Connection," appears in the May–June 1999 issue of *Naval History* magazine, published by the U.S. Naval Institute at Annapolis, Maryland. Borgquist points out that a Mrs. Helen E. Hamman wrote a letter to President Clinton, dated September 5, 1995, when she heard that the families of Admiral Kimmel and General Short were trying to clear their names in the Pearl Harbor matter. She reported that she was the daughter of Mr. Don C. Smith who died in 1990 at the age of 98. Mr. Smith directed the War Service for the Red Cross before World War II, and he informed his daughter during the 1970s that he had worried for years about the fact that he had been called to the White House shortly before the Pearl Harbor attack in 1941 and had a personal meeting with President Roosevelt. The letter of Mrs. Hamman states the following account of the meeting:

> Shortly before the attack in 1941, President Roosevelt called him [Smith] to the White House for a meeting concerning a Top Secret matter. At this meeting the president advised my

father that his intelligence staff had informed him of a pending attack on Pearl Harbor, by the Japanese. He [FDR] anticipated many casualties and much loss; he instructed my father to send workers and supplies to a holding area . . . on the West Coast. When he protested to the president, President Roosevelt told him that the American people would never agree to enter the war in Europe unless they were attack[ed] within their own borders. . . . He followed the orders of the president and spent many years contemplating this action which he considered ethically and morally wrong.

Borgquist reports that the Red Cross records indicate a substantial supply of personnel and medical equipment was sent by the Red Cross to Hawaii shortly before the Pearl Harbor attack.

A huge monument has been erected in Washington, D.C., to celebrate the "greatness" of President Franklin D. Roosevelt. On the monument is a quotation from Roosevelt—"I hate war"—indicating falsely to the public that he was a president who sought peace rather than war. It is an example of false propaganda that is being perpetrated upon the American people. We learn from the investigation of the Pearl Harbor matter that after the attack ended, some of the crew of the battleship Oklahoma were still alive and trapped inside the hull of the partially sunken ship. The survivors outside could hear the trapped men knocking against the hull with metal objects desperately seeking rescue, but no rescue was possible (Beach, *Scapegoats*, p. 111). A recording should be made to duplicate their desperate sounds and have it played every hour at the Roosevelt Memorial to remind Americans of the treachery of their commander-in-chief.

RECOMMENDED READINGS

Alperovitz, Gar. 1995. *The Decision to Use the Atomic Bomb*. New York: Vintage Books, A Division of Random House.

Bacque, James. 1997. *Crimes and Mercies: The Fate of German Civilians Under Allied Occupations, 1944–1950*. London: Little Brown.

Barnes, Harry Elmer. [1926] 1980. *Revisionism: A Key to Peace and Other Essays*. San Francisco: Cato Institute.

———. [1926] 1970. *Genesis of The World War: An Introduction to the Problem of Guilt*. New York: Howard Fertig.

———. 1928. *In Quest of Truth and Justice*. Chicago: National Historical Society.

———. 1969. *Perpetual War for Perpetual Peace*. New York: Greenwood Press.

———. 1992. *Pearl Harbor After a Quarter of a Century*. New York: Arno Press.

Beard, Charles A. 1939. *Giddy Minds and Foreign Quarrels*. New York: McMillan.

———. 1940. *A Foreign Policy for America*. New York: Alfred A. Knopf.

———. 1946. *American Foreign Policy in the Making, 1932–1940*. New Haven, Conn.: Yale University Press.

———. 1948. *President Roosevelt and the Coming of the War, 1941*. New Haven, Conn.: Yale University Press.

Bensel, Richard Franklin. 1990. *Yankee Leviathan: The Origins of the Central State Authority in America, 1859–1877*. New York: Cambridge University Press.

Chamberlin, William H. 1962. *America's Second Crusade*. Colorado Springs, Colo.: Ralph Myles.

Cochran, M.H. 1972. *Germany Not Guilty 1914*. Colorado Springs, Colo.: Ralph Myles.

Colby, Benjamin. 1974. *'Twas a Famous Victory: Deception and Propaganda in the War Against Germany*. New York: Arlington House.

DiLorenzo, Thomas J. 2002. *The Real Lincoln: A New Look at Abraham Lincoln, His Agenda and An Unnecessary War*. Roseville, Calif.: Prima Publishing Company, A Division of Random House.

Doenecke, Justus D. 1972. *The Literature of Isolationism: A Guide to Non-Interventionist Scholarship, 1930–1972*. Colorado Springs, Colo.: Ralph Myles.

Dwyer, John J. 2005. *The War Between the States: America's Uncivil War*. Denton, Texas: Bonnett Press.

Eland, Ivan. 2004. *The Empire Has No Clothes: U.S. Foreign Policy Exposed*. Oakland, Calif.: The Independent Institute.

Fleming, Thomas. 2001. *The New Dealers' War: F.D.R. and the War Within World War II*. New York: Basic Books, Perseus Books Group.

———. 2003. *The Illusion of Victory, America in World War I*. New York: Basic Books, Perseus Books Group.

Flynn, John T. 1973. *As We Go Marching*. New York: Free Life.

Garrett, Garet. 1953. "Rise of Empire." In *The People's Pottage*. Caldwell, Idaho: Caxton.

Goddard, Arthur, ed. 1968. *Harry Elmer Barnes, Learned Crusader: New History in Action*. Colorado Springs, Colo.: Ralph Myles.

Hummel, Jeffrey Rogers. 1996. *Emancipating Slaves, Enslaving Free Men: A History of The American Civil War*. Chicago and LaSalle, Illinois: Open Court.

Johnson, Chalmers. 2000. *Blowback: The Costs and Consequences of American Empire*. New York: Henry Holt and Company.

———. 2004. *The Sorrows of Empire: Militarism, Secrecy and the End of The Republic*. New York: Metropolitan Books, Henry Holt and Company.

Kinzer, Stephen. 2006. *Overthrow: America's Century Regime Change from Hawaii to Iraq*. New York: Henry Holt.

Martin, James J. 1963. *American Liberalism and World Politics*. Old Greenwich, Conn.: Devin-Adair.

———. 1971. *Revisionist Viewpoints: Essays in a Dissident Historical Tradition*. Colorado Springs, Colo.: Ralph Myles.

Morgenstern, George. 1947. *Pearl Harbor: The Story of The Secret War*. Old Greenwich, Conn.: Devin-Adair.

Neilson, Francis. 1915. *How Diplomats Make War*. San Francisco: Cobden Press.

———. 1987. *The Makers of War*. New Orleans: Flanders Hall.

Ponsonby, Arthur. 1928. *Falsehood in Wartime*. New York: E.P. Dutton.

Ponting, Clive. 1990. *1940: Myth and Reality*. Chicago: Ivan R. Dee.

Powell, Jim. 2005. *Wilson's War: How Woodrow Wilson's Great Blunder Led to Hitler, Lenin, Stalin and World War II*. New York: Crown Forum-Random House.

Ravenal, Earl C. 1978. *Never Again: Learning from America's Foreign Policy Failures*. Philadelphia: Temple University Press.

Russett, Bruce M. 1972. *No Clear and Present Danger: A Skeptical View of the United States Entry Into World War II*. New York: Harper and Rowe.

Scheur, Michael. 2004. *Imperial Hubris: Why the West is Losing the War on Terror*. Washington, D.C.: Brassey's.

Taft, Robert. 1951. *A Foreign Policy for Americans*. Garden City, N.Y.: Doubleday.

Tansill, Charles C. [1938] 1963. *America Goes to War*. Gloucester, Mass.: Peter Smith.

———. 1952. *Backdoor to War: The Roosevelt Foreign Policy, 1933–1941*. Chicago: Regnery.

Taylor, A.J.P. 1961. *The Origins of the Second World War*. Second Edition. Old Greenwich, Conn.: Faucet Premier Books.

Tilley, John Shippley. 1991. *Lincoln Takes Command*. Nashville, Tenn.: Bill Coats.

Veale, F.J.P. 1968. *Advance to Barbarism: A Re-examination*. Old Greenwich, Conn.: Devin-Adair.

Weiner, Tim. 2007. *Legacy of Ashes: History of the CIA*. New York: Doubleday.

BIBLIOGRAPHY

Acton, Lord, *Essays in the History of Liberty: Selected Writings of Lord Acton*, J. Rufus Fears, ed. (Indianapolis, Ind.: Liberty Classics, 1985), vol. 1.

Adams, Charles, *When In The Course of Human Events: Arguing the Case for Southern Secession* (Lanham, Md.: Rowman and Littlefield, 2000).

——. *For Good and Evil: The Impact of Taxes on the Course of Civilization*, 2nd ed. (New York: Madison Books, 1999).

——. *Those Dirty Rotten Taxes: The Tax Revolts that Built America* (New York: The Free Press, 1998), pp. 81–112.

——, and Brandes, Stuart D. *Wardogs: A History of War Profits in America* (Lexington: University Press of Kentucky, 1997).

Bailey, Thomas A., *Presidential Greatness: The Image and the Man from George Washington to the Present* (New York: Appleman Century-Crofts, 1966).

——. *The Man in the Street: The Impact of American Public Opinion on Foreign Policy* (New York: Macmillan, 1948).

Barnes, Harry Elmer, "Revisionism and the Historical Blackout," in *Perpetual War for Perpetual Peace: A Critical Examination of the Foreign Policy of Franklin Delano Roosevelt and Its Aftermath*, Harry Elmer Barnes, ed. (New York: Greenwood Press, 1969).

Bartlett, John, *Familiar Quotations*, Emily Morrison Beck, ed., 14th ed. (Boston: Little, Brown, 1968).

Bartlett, Bruce R., *Cover-Up: The Politics of Pearl Harbor, 1941–1946* (New Rochelle, N.Y.: Arlington House, 1978).

Beach, Edward L. (Captain, USN Ret.), *Scapegoats: A Defense of Kimmel and Short at Pearl Harbor* (Annapolis, Md.: Naval Institute Press, 1995).

Beale, Howard K., *Diary of Gideon Welles: Secretary of Navy Under Lincoln and Johnson* (New York: Norton, 1960), vol. 1.

Bethell, Nicholas, *The Last Secret: The Delivery to Stalin of Over Two Million Russians by Britain and the United States* (New York: Basic Books, 1974).

Borgquist, Daryl S., "Advance Warning: The Red Cross Connection," *Naval History* (May–June 1999).

Boritt, Gabor S., "War Opponent and War President," in *Lincoln The War President: The Gettysburg Lectures,* Gabor S. Boritt, ed. (New York: Oxford University Press, 1992).

Brody, J. Kenneth, *The Avoidable War: Lord Cecil and the Policy of Principle—1933–1935* (New Brunswick, N.J.: Transaction Publishers, 1999), vol. 1.

Buchanan, Pat, *A Republic, Not an Empire: Reclaiming America's Destiny* (Washington, D.C.: Regnery, 1999).

Bullitt, William C., and Sigmund Freud, *Woodrow Wilson: A Psychological Study* (New Brunswick, N.J.: Transaction Publishers, [1967] 1999).

Bullock, Alan, *Hitler, A Study in Tyranny* (New York: Harper and Row 1962).

Casey, William, *The Secret War Against Hitler* (Washington, D.C.: Regnery Gateway, 1988).

Catton, Bruce, *The Coming Fury* (Garden City, N.Y.: Doubleday, 1961).

Churchill, Winston, *The Second World War*, vol. 3: *The Grand Alliance* (Boston: Houghton Mifflin, 1950).

Cochran, M.H., *Germany Not Guilty in 1914* (Colorado Springs, Colo.: Ralph Myles, 1972).

Colby, Benjamin, *'Twas a Famous Victory: Deception and Propaganda in the War Against Germany* (New Rochelle, N.Y.: Arlington House, 1974).

Robert Conquest, *The Great Terror: Stalin's Purge of the Thirties* (New York: Macmillan, 1968).

———. *The Harvest of Sorrow: Soviet Collectivization and the Terror-Famine* (New York: Oxford University Press, 1986).

Crocker, George N., *Roosevelt's Road to Russia* (Chicago: Henry Regnery, 1959).

Current, Richard N., *Lincoln and The First Shot* (Prospect Heights, Ill.: Waveland Press, 1963).

Dabney, Robert L., "Memoir of a Narrative Received of Colonel John B. Baldwin of Staunton, Touching the Origin of the War," *Discussions* (Harrisonburg, Va.: Sprinkle Publications, 1994).

Davis, Jefferson, *Rise and Fall of the Confederate Government* (Nashville, Tenn: William Mayes Coats, 1996), vol. 1.

Davis, William C., *A Government of Our Own: The Making of the Confederacy* (New York: The Free Press, 1994).

Degler, Carl N. "The United States and National Unification," in *Lincoln the War President: The Gettysburg Lectures*, Gabor S. Boritt, ed. (New York: Oxford University Press, 1992).

Denson, John V., "War and American Freedom," in *The Costs of War: America's Pyrrhic Victories*, John V. Denson, ed., 2nd ed. (New Brunswick, N.J.: Transaction Publishers, 1999).

DiLorenzo, Thomas J., "Yankee Confederates: New England Secessionists Movement Prior to the War Between the States," in *Secession, State and Liberty*, David Gordon, ed. (New Brunswick, N.J.: Transaction Publishers, 1998).

Douglas, Gregory, *Gestapo Chief: The 1948 Interrogation of Heinrich Müller* (San Jose, Calif.: R. James Bender, 1998), vol. 3.

Engdahl, F. William, *A Century of War: Anglo-American Oil Politics and the New World Order* (Concord, Mass.: Paul and Company, 1993).

Fears, J. Rufus, ed., *Essays in the History of Liberty, Selected Writings of Lord Acton* (Indianapolis, Ind: Liberty Fund, 1985), vol. 1.

Ferguson, Niall, *The Pity of War* (London: Allen Lane, Penguin Press, 1998).

———. *Virtual History: Alternatives and Counterfactuals* (London: Papermac, [1977] 1997).

Foner, Phillip S., *Business and Slavery: The New York Merchants and The Irrepressible Conflict* (Chapel Hill, N.C.: Duke University Press. 1941).

Foote, Shelby, *The Civil War: A Narrative, Fort Sumter to Perryville* (New York: Vintage Books, 1986).

Forster, Stig, and Gorg Nagler, eds., *On the Road to Total War: The American Civil War and the German Wars of Unification, 1861–1871* (Washington, D.C.: German Historical Institute and Cambridge University Press, 1997).

Gordon, David, "A Common Design: Propaganda and World War," in *The Costs of War: America's Pyrrhic Victories*, John V. Denson, ed., 2nd ed. (New Brunswick, N.J.: Transaction Publishers, 1999).

———, ed. *Secession, State and Liberty*, (New Brunswick, N.J.: Transaction Publishers, 1998).

Gutzman, K.R. Constantine, "'Oh, What a Tangled Web We Weave . . .': James Madison and the Compound Republic," *Continuity: A Journal of History* 22 (1998).

Greenstein, Fred I., ed., *Leadership in the Modern Presidency* (Cambridge, Mass.: Harvard University Press, 1988).

Harman, Nicholas, *Dunkirk: The Patriotic Myth* (New York: Simon and Schuster, 1980).

Harris, Air Marshall Sir Arthur, *Bomber Offensive* (London: Kimber, 1963).

Hayek, F.A. *The Collected Works of F.A. Hayek*, vol. 10: *Socialism and War: Essays, Documents, Reviews*, Bruce Caldwell, ed. (Chicago: University of Chicago Press, 1997).

Hoopes, Towsend, and Douglas Brinkley, *FDR and the Creation of the U.N.* (New Haven, Conn.: Yale University Press, 1997).

Hunt, Gaillard, and James Brown Scott, eds., *The Debates in the Federal Convention of 1787 Which Framed the Constitution of the United States of America* (Buffalo, N.Y.: Prometheus Books, 1987), vol. 2.

Hyde, H. Montgomery, *The Quiet Canadian: The Secret Service Story of Sir William Stephenson* (London: Hamish Hamilton, 1963).

Irving, David, *Churchill's War: The Struggle for Power* (Western Australia: Veritas, 1987), vol. 1.

Johnson, Paul, "Why Britain Should Join America," *Forbes* (April 5, 1999).

Jordon, George R. (Maj. USAF), *From Major Jordan's Diaries* (New York: Harcourt, Brace, 1952).

Keller, Werner, *Are the Russians Ten Feet Tall?* Constantine FitzGibbon, trans. (London: Thames and Hudson, 1961).

Kubek, Anthony, *How the Far East Was Lost: American Policy and the Creation of Communist China, 1941–1949* (Chicago: Henry Regnery, 1963).

Kuehnelt-Leddihn, Erik von, *Leftism Revisited: From de Sade and Marx to Hitler and Pol Pot* (Washington, D.C.: Regnery Gateway, 1990).

Lincoln, Abraham, *The Collected Works of Abraham Lincoln*, Roy P. Basler, ed. (New Brunswick, N.J.: Rutgers University Press, 1953–55), vol. 1.

Link, Arthur S., ed., *The Papers of Woodrow Wilson* (Princeton, N.J.: Princeton University Press, 1990), vol. 63.

Livingston, Donald W., "The Secession Tradition in America," in *Secession, State and Liberty*, David Gordon, ed. (New Brunswick, N.J.: Transaction Publishers, 1998).

Madison, James, "Political Observations," *Letters and Other Writings of James Madison (1795)* (Philadelphia: J.B. Lippincott, 1865), vol. 4.

Mahl, Thomas E., *Desperate Deception: British Covert Operations in the United States, 1939–44* (Washington, D.C.: Brassey's, 1998).

Marshall, John A., *American Bastile: A History of the Illegal Arrests and Imprisonment of American Citizens in the Northern and Border States, on Account of Their Political Opinions, During the Late Civil War* (Wiggins, Miss.: Crown Rights, [1881] 1998).

Masters, Edgar Lee, *Lincoln, The Man* (Columbia, S.C.: The Foundation for American Education, 1997).

May, Christopher N., *In the Name of War: Judicial Review and the War Powers Since 1918* (Cambridge, Mass.: Harvard University Press, 1989).

McDonald, Forrest, *The American Presidency* (Lawrence: University Press of Kansas, 1994).

Minor, Charles L.C., in M.D. Carter, *The Real Lincoln: From the Testimony of His Contemporaries*, 4th ed. (Harrisonburg, Va.: Sprinkle Publications, 1992).

Mises, Ludwig von, *Omnipotent Government: The Rise of the Total State and Total War* (New Rochelle, N.Y.: Arlington House, 1969).

Morgenstern, George, *Pearl Harbor: The Story of the Secret War* (Old Greenwich, Conn.: Devin-Adair, 1947).

Morley, Felix, *The Foreign Policy of the United States* (New York: Alfred A. Knopf, 1951).

Murray, Robert, and Tim H. Blessing, "The Presidential Performance Study: A Progress Report," *Journal of American History* 70 (December 1983).

Mussolini, Benito, "The Political and Social Doctrine of Fascism," in *Fascism: An Anthology*, Nathanael Greene, ed. (New York: Thomas Y. Crowell, 1968).

Neelly, Jr., Mark E., *The Fate of Liberty: Abraham Lincoln and Civil Liberties* (New York and Oxford: Oxford University Press, 1991).

Nevin, John, *Gideon Welles, Lincoln's Secretary of Navy* (Baton Rouge: Louisiana State University Press, 1994).

Nevins, Allan, *Henry White: Thirty Years of American Diplomacy* (New York: Harper and Brothers, 1930).

Nielson, Francis, *The Makers of War* (New Orleans, La.: Flanders Hall, 1987).

Nock, Albert Jay, *The State of the Union: Essays in Social Criticism* (Indianapolis, Ind.: Liberty Press, 1991).

Perkins, Howard Cecil, ed., *Northern Editorials on Secession* (Gloucester, Mass: Peter Smith, 1964), vol. 2.

Perlmutter, Amos, *FDR and Stalin: A Not So Grand Alliance, 1943–1944* (Columbia: University of Missouri Press, 1993).

Porter, Bruce D., *War and the Rise of the State: The Military Foundations of Modern Politics* (New York: Free Press, 1994).

Potter, David M., Lincoln and His Party in the Secession Crisis (Baton Rouge: Louisiana State University Press, 1995).

Quigley, Carroll, *The Anglo-American Establishment: From Rhodes to Cliveden* (New York: Books in Focus, 1981).

——. *Tragedy and Hope: A History of the World in Our Time* (New York: Macmillan, 1974).

Raico, Ralph, "Re-Thinking Churchill," in *The Costs of War: America's Pyrrhic Victories*, John V. Denson, ed., 2nd ed. (New Brunswick, N.J.: Transaction Publishers, 1999).

Ramsdell, Charles W., "Lincoln and Fort Sumter," *The Journal of Southern History* 3 (Southern Historical Association, February–November, 1937).

Randall, James G., *Constitutional Problems Under Lincoln* (Chicago: University of Chicago Press, 1951).

Richardson, James O., *On the Treadmill to Pearl Harbor: The Memoirs of Admiral James O. Richardson USN (Ret.) as told to Vice Admiral George C. Dyer, USN (Ret.)* (Washington, D.C.: Naval History Division, Department of Navy, 1973).

Rothbard, Murray N., *Wall Street, Banks, and American Foreign Policy* (Burlingame, Calif.: Center for Libertarian Studies, 1995).

Rummel, R.J., *Power Kills: Democracy as a Method of Nonviolence* (New Brunswick, N.J.: Transaction Publishers, 1997).

——. *Death by Government* (New Brunswick, N.J.: Transaction Publishers, 1995).

Rusbridger, James, and Eric Nave, *Betrayal at Pearl Harbor: How Churchill Lured Roosevelt into World War II* (New York: Summit Books, 1991).

Schlesinger, Jr., Arthur M., "War and the Constitution: Abraham Lincoln and Franklin D. Roosevelt," in *Lincoln The War President: The Gettysburg Lectures*, Gabor S. Boritt, ed. (New York: Oxford University Press, 1992).

——. *The Imperial Presidency* (Boston: Houghton Mifflin, 1973).

Simpson, Colin, *The Lusitania* (New York: Ballantine Books, 1974).

Snow, John Holland, *The Case of Tyler Kent* (New Canaan, Conn.: The Long House, 1982).

Spaight, James E., *Bombing Vindicated* (London: G. Bles, 1944).

Stampp, Kenneth M., *And the War Came: The North and the Secession Crisis, 1860–1861* (Baton Rouge: Louisiana State University Press, 1990).

Stephens, Alexander H., *A Constitutional View of the War Between the States* (Harrisonburg, Va.: Sprinkle Publications, 1994), vol. 2.

Stevenson, William, *A Man Called Intrepid: The Secret War* (New York: Ballantine Books, 1976).

Stinnett, Robert B., *Day of Deceit: The Truth about FDR and Pearl Harbor* (New York: The Free Press, 2000).

Swanberg, W.A., *First Blood: The Story of Fort Sumter* (New York: Charles Scribener's Sons, 1957).

Talbert, Bart Rhett, *Maryland: The South's First Casualty* (Berryville, Va.: Rockbridge, 1995).

Tansill, Charles Callan, "The United States and the Road to War in Europe," in *Perpetual War for Perpetual Peace: A Critical Examination of the Foreign Policy of Franklin Delano Roosevelt and Its Aftermath*, Harry Elmer Barnes, ed. (New York: Greenwood Press, 1969).

Taussig, Frank, *The Tariff History of the United States* (New York: Putnam, 1931).

Taylor, A.J.P., *The Origins of the Second World War*, 2nd ed. (Greenwich, Conn.: Fawcett Publications, 1961).

Tilley, John Shipley, *Lincoln Takes Command* (Nashville, Tenn.: Bill Coats, 1991).

Tolley, Kemp, *Cruise of the Lanikai: Incitement to War* (Annapolis, Md.: Naval Institute Press, 1973).

Tocqueville, Alexis de, *Democracy in America* (New York: Alfred A. Knopf, 1980), vol. 2.

Van der Linden, Frank, *Lincoln: The Road to War* (Golden, Colo.: Fulcrum Publishing, 1998).

———. *Lincoln: The Road to War* (Golden, Colo.: Fulcrum Publishing, 1998).

Van Doren, Carl, ed., "First Inaugural Address," *The Literary Works of Abraham Lincoln* (Norwalk, Conn.: Easton Press, 1970).

Washington, George, *George Washington: A Collection*, W.B. Allen, ed. (Indianapolis, Ind.: Liberty Classics, 1988).

Weintraub, Stanley, *Silent Night: The Story of The World War I Christmas Truce* (New York: Penguin Putnam, 2002).

Wheeler-Bennett, John W., *King George VI: His Life and Reign* (New York: St. Martin's, 1958).

Wilson, Woodrow, *The Papers of Woodrow Wilson*, Arthur S. Link, ed. (Princeton, N.J.: Princeton University Press, 1990), vol. 63.

Zakaria, Fareed, *From Wealth to Power: The Unusual Origins of America's World Role* (Princeton, N.J.: Princeton University Press, 1998).

INDEX

31869931R00121

Made in the USA
Middletown, DE
02 January 2019